A VERY SHORT,
FAIRLY INTERESTING AND
REASONABLY CHEAP BOOK ABOUT
STUDYING MARKETING

D0817214

A VERY SHORT, FAIRLY INTERESTING AND REASONABLY CHEAP BOOK ABOUT STUDYING MARKETING

JIM BLYTHE

SAGE Publications

London ● Thousand Oaks ● New Delhi

SAGE Publications Ltd
1 Oliver's Yard
55 City Road
London EC1Y 1SP

SAGE Publications Inc.
2455 Teller Road
Thousand Oaks, California 91320

SAGE Publications India Pvt Ltd
B-42, Panchsheel Enclave
Post Box 4109
New Delhi 110 017

British Library Cataloguing in Publication data

A catalogue record for this book is available
from the British Library

ISBN-10 1-4129-3087-1   ISBN-13 978-1-4129-3087-1
ISBN-10 1-4129-3088-X   ISBN-13 978-1-4129-3088-8 (pbk)

Library of Congress Control Number: 2006925228

Typeset by C&M Digitals (P) Ltd, Chennai, India
Printed and bound in Great Britain by Athenaeum Press, Gateshead
Printed on paper from sustainable resources

Contents

Contents

Introduction: Studying Marketing

I wouldn't necessarily say that marketing has always fascinated me, and it's quite possible that I will get bored with it eventually and move on to some other field of human endeavour – it wouldn't be the first time. But for the past twenty years or more I have been involved in marketing one way or another.

I have sold stuff, run businesses, been a consultant, been a hands-on marketer for various companies, and latterly I have been teaching the stuff. Marketing is still fascinating, because essentially it's about people, and it brings in so many aspects of people's lives because it's about how we meet our needs.

When I first started to teach marketing I was painfully aware of how little I knew about the theoretical aspects of the subject. As an undergraduate doing a business degree, I found that my marketing lecturers were so laid back that they were somnolent and we, as the students, had absolutely no idea what marketing was or what it could do for us. Luckily, the gentlemen in question did not hold our lack of knowledge against us at exam time and we all passed without too much difficulty, although I have to say my profound ignorance of marketing turned round and bit me once I actually went out and got a job. I knew virtually nothing.

As an academic, with some years' experience in the job and with a suitable string of publications, I still have twinges about how much I don't know about the subject. At conferences everyone seems to know so much more than I do, and to have actually read all the papers, and to understand long words better than I do. Maybe that's a feature of conferences, of course, but I think it's also a general problem with knowledge – the more you know, the more you realize how much more there is to learn. Luckily, learning is like eating peanuts–easy to start, but difficult to stop.

So it is with this book. This is not a textbook as such, it will not provide you with everything you need to pass a course in marketing. There are plenty of those around. In fact, there are several of mine out there which I would really like you to buy. What this book is intended to do is give you some of my favourite ideas (mine and other people's) on the study of the phenomenon of marketing, and to point out some of the pitfalls of believing everything you read. It is also intended to be the first peanut in the knowledge-nibbling process.

If this were a textbook, I would now be wishing you good luck with your studies. Since it isn't, I would like to express the hope that you enjoy the book: see it as a bit of light relief. The drawback of formal education is that it takes all the fun out of learning – luckily, my two marketing lecturers ensured that I had no formal learning of marketing, so like a road sweeper I have picked it up as I went along, and consequently I learned it for fun. I recommend you to do the same.

Part I

Proper Subjects that Preceded Marketing

The Economists

In 1776, the year of the start of the American War of Independence, a Scotsman called Adam Smith published a remarkable book. It was called *An Inquiry into the Nature and Causes of the Wealth of Nations*, and it set out to explain how countries become wealthy. The lengthy title is usually condensed to simply *Wealth of Nations* nowadays, but the ideas within the book are still well-regarded to this day (Smith, 1998 [1776]). Smith's liking for lengthy titles extended into the book itself. It is subdivided into five books, totalling 32 chapters in all, and although each chapter is fairly short, the book is a substantial one which seeks to encompass all aspects of wealth creation.

Smith's work is important because it was the first book to be written about economics: it is interesting because it says a lot about life in the eighteenth century. For instance, Smith uses the example of pin manufacture, explaining the eighteenth-century process in considerable detail in order to show how division of labour increases efficiency. In Chapter Two of Book One, Smith outlines the basis of the marketing concept, as follows:

> But man has almost constant occasion for the help of his brethren, and it is in vain for him to expect it from their benevolence only. He will be more likely to prevail if he can interest their self-love in his favour, and show them that it is for their own advantage to do for him what he requires of them. Whoever offers to another a bargain of any kind, proposes to do this. Give me that which I want, and you shall have this which you want, is the meaning of every such offer, and it is in this manner that we obtain from one another the far greater part of those good offices which we stand in need of. It is not from the benevolence of the butcher, the brewer or the baker that we expect our dinner, but from their regard to their own interest.

The marketing concept essentially says that the route to success is to consider the customer's needs – which is exactly what Adam Smith was telling us 230 years ago. Smith saw self-interested exchange as one of the cornerstones of developing wealth in nations, and for developing the wealth of individuals. This is a concept which certainly has resonances for modern marketers – the idea that marketing delivers a standard of living was widespread in the 1960s and 1970s. Indeed, for many marketers the whole basis of marketing is the management of exchange.

Smith's ideas became the basis for the Classical school of economics (replacing the early Mercantilist and Physiocratic schools). Classical economics took the view that the 'invisible hand' of the marketplace would ultimately result in the greatest good for the greatest number, because each person would ensure his or her own welfare by exchanging with others: provided the exchanges were fair, the end result would be an increase in everyone's wealth. Smith suggested that three basic factors of production (land, labour and capital) could be combined in different ways to create wealth, and that (in the long run, at least) these factors would be combined in the most efficient way possible, since that would be in everybody's best interests. Later economists included the idea that entrepreneurship is also a factor of production: the willingness to risk one's own capital and creative effort in the hope of future rewards is essential if businesses are to start up and to prosper.

Smith also believed that a free marketplace would lead to full employment, and that government intervention in the marketplace (which had been advocated by the Mercantilists) would lead to distortions, thus reducing the efficiency of the market in creating wealth for everyone.

Not surprisingly, these ideas were warmly greeted by merchants and landowners. There has probably never been a time when business people didn't want to get the government off their backs, and following on from the radical intervention of government during the Mercantilist period (when governments applied huge tariffs to anything imported, and offered huge subsidies to anything which could be exported) Smith must have been a hero to the businessmen of his day.

greed is good

Gordon Gecko, in the film *Wall Street*, famously said 'The point is, ladies and gentlemen, greed is good. Greed works, greed is right ... and greed, mark my words, will save not only Teldar Paper but the other malfunctioning corporation called the USA.' Smith could have written those words himself. But how true is this idea?

As is almost always the case with a one-solution argument, the frame of the picture has been drawn too small. Not everybody knows what's good for them, for example. Some people are poor negotiators. Some exchanges are fraudulent. Some people have more power in the relationship than others – an idea put forward by a later economist, David Ricardo, who pointed out that we don't have unlimited land, and therefore landowners will experience a steady increase in the value of their land as demand increases (Ricardo, 1992 [1817]). Two hundred years later marketers are still struggling with the concept that exchange is not always fair or good for the consumer – we know that it's easy to sell people products which are unhealthy, environmentally damaging, or socially unacceptable but are we morally justified in doing so? According to Gordon Gecko (and Adam Smith), there is no problem, because greed is good. In which case we might as well all become drug dealers and pornographers, because that's where the money is.

Before you rush off to start a new career, it may be worth considering the contributions of later economists. Ricardo has already had a mention for explaining that landowners have more power in the relationship than either capital or labour. Following on from this idea, Thomas Malthus (1992 [1798]) put forward the proposition that rising population would mean that limited resources would quickly be exhausted – population increases geometrically, whereas other resources only increase arithmetically. According to Malthus, we should all have starved to death long ago, which of course has not happened (at least in wealthy countries) because our population has stabilized and in any case our production of food has become much greater than anticipated. The basic principle remains, though, that the planet has only finite resources and (whether there are more of us or not) we are consuming those resources at an increasing rate. Malthus may have been replaced by Friends of the Earth, but the Cassandra-like warnings are growing ever louder.

Ricardo and Malthus filled in some of the gaps in Smith's thinking, and (of course) complicated the model quite a lot by adding a moral and ethical dimension. Some marketers (notably Kotler) have put forward the idea that marketers need to be socially responsible, and consider the long-term welfare of the customers. This concept has been expressed as 'societal marketing' – a lovely idea, but one which might be difficult to push through at a board meeting.

The drawbacks of classical economics became painfully clear as the nineteenth century rolled on. Wealth became concentrated in the hands of capitalists and landowners, and wages were screwed down as low as the employers could manage – there was plenty of labour around, but land was no more plentiful than it had been since the Ice Age, and capitalists held the purse-strings and controlled the means of production. This led to the economists having a bit of a re-think. The leading thinker on this issue was, of course, Karl Marx. Marx was a German living in London, and he saw all about him the effects of the laissez-faire, Smith-type classical economics. Non-intervention by government had not led, as Smith had thought, to the greatest wealth of the greatest number, but had instead created poverty and misery for the bulk of the population, and fabulous wealth for a few. Marx believed that capitalism would eventually destroy itself, because wealth was created by labour and eventually the starving masses would rise up and overthrow their masters, making private property obsolete in a world where the workers ran things (Marx, 1993 [1867]).

Marxist thinking created the great Communist countries of the twentieth century, and encouraged revolutionaries everywhere to rise up against the capitalists. It would be interesting to find out if Marxism could ever work: it was only ever tried in agricultural economies, never in a modern industrialized state, so we may never know the answer. I always thought Marx was a brave soul, but with fatally-flawed thinking: he thought he had discovered the laws of history, but in fact there are no laws because people are just making things up as they go along. His belief that labour added value to raw materials did not take account of the idea of a bad workman, for instance – those of us who have been employers know that there are some people whom we should pay to stay at home, because they cause more damage than they are worth if they show up for work. He also ignored a factor which became the fourth element of classical economics: enterprise.

Enterprise is the willingness to take a risk, and it is an essential part of any business activity, especially in start-ups. Being prepared to back a new idea or a new product with hard cash and personal effort is what makes things happen, but this did not figure in Marx's thinking. Sitting in the British Museum Library (which is where he wrote *Das Kapital*, his monumental work on capitalism) he was probably not exactly in the entrepreneurial hotbed of London.

So far most economists had been thinking about wealth and welfare from a somewhat lofty plane – their thinking was about ways to increase the wealth of the country as a whole, and how economic policies could be applied to everything in order to create the right conditions for prosperity. Few of them had considered what happens at the level of the individual person or company. In other words, they had invented macroeconomics before inventing microeconomics. This may seem a little odd in view of the fact that the word 'economics' is derived from a Greek word meaning 'housekeeping'.

Classical economists had theorized that prices are determined by the costs of production. This may have been the case in the eighteenth century, but it is certainly not the case nowadays. The thinking was that suppliers would produce goods as cheaply as they could, then add on a profit margin and offer the products for sale. Most of us tend to think this is still largely the case, and most accountants and engineers use this approach when they calculate prices, using cost-plus pricing. This self-centred view of the exchange process leaves out half the equation, namely the customers, despite Smith's declaration that 'the customer is king'. What Marginalist economists (represented by Alfred Marshall and Leon Walras) contributed was that prices are also determined by demand.

This may seem obvious now, but was not quite so obvious in the nineteenth century. Alfred Marshall (1997 [1890]) developed a complex mathematical proof for the laws of supply and demand – in order to tell us that if something is too expensive, people won't buy it, but if it is cheap they will buy more of it. Not exactly rocket science, but it is one of the key concepts of microeconomics. The 'pile it high and sell it cheap' school of marketing certainly has its adherents, but (as is always the case with economic, or any other, models) the frame is too small to show the whole picture. Walras, who was an economics professor at the University of Lausanne, felt himself to be on the periphery of economic thought. At the time, most economists were based in the UK, so Walras had to say something pretty profound to get himself noticed. What he actually came out with was a general equilibrium theory, which demonstrated mathematically that economies would naturally find an equilibrium in which the prices of commodities were stable (Walras, 1984 [1874]). In fact, the theory had more holes in it than a string vest, but later economists plugged many of the holes and Walras is now regarded as a major contributor to the field.

Where Marshall and Walras went slightly adrift is by postulating that competing products are identical, and that everyone has perfect knowledge of the marketplace. To put it as kindly as possible, these two assumptions do not easily transfer into the real world. It may be true that mackerel caught by two competing fishermen have little to choose between them, and therefore the fishermen would have to charge more or less the same price, but the same is not true of sausages, cheeses, Bird's Eye ready meals, cars, books, or indeed anything with some kind of manufacturing to add value to it. Marx would have loved the idea of product differentiation – it is proof positive that adding more labour to something increases its value.

The other assumption, perfect knowledge, also does not stand up to close scrutiny. Even if one has perfect knowledge (for example, by using the Internet to make comparisons), this does not translate readily into an ability to do something about it. Knowing that a second-hand Ford Mondeo can be bought for £300 less from a dealer in Sheffield does not help much if one happens to live in Penzance. Equally, knowing that one plumber can fix a burst pipe for £20 less than the plumber who is currently working on the pipe is no help if it is three in the morning and the kitchen is flooded. In practice, of course, perfect knowledge (like the perfect England football team) does not actually exist, however pleasant and intellectually satisfying it might be to discuss the possibility among friends.

Another interesting idea from the Marginalists was that capital, labour and land would each receive their proper reward according to their contribution to the finished product. This is a peculiar proposition, because it seems to imply that there is some kind of automatic process involved – perhaps the invisible hand of the market – and that people are powerless to change it. In practice, of course, people negotiate (or even cheat a bit) in order to increase their personal welfare at the expense of others. The main effect of the Marginalist view of reward is that those who were most successful at grabbing the loot for themselves were able to justify their rapacity with a solid academic argument – hurrah for marginalism. Like Smith before them, the Marginalists were (understandably) the darlings of the 'haves' while Marxist economists were beloved by the 'have nots'.

Being able to put an acceptable face on the concept of greed is understandable, of course. When one's friends ask what you do for a living, 'Grind the faces of the poor' is not the right answer. 'Generate wealth and jobs for the poor' sounds a lot better.

'it's the economy, stupid!'

During the 1992 American Presidential election, Bill Clinton needed reminding that the US economy was going to be a key issue in the campaign. His strategist, James Carville, put up a sign in Clinton's campaign headquarters which said simply, 'The economy, stupid!' to remind Clinton to stay focused on economic issues.

Governments love to intervene (or interfere, depending on your viewpoint) in the economy because of the remarkable effect it has on voters. Everybody wants the economy to grow, because growth means more wealth to be divided up: once we have created a bit of wealth, everybody has an interest in how it is divided. Governments throughout the world feel an irrepressible urge to tinker with things, and of course because governments set the taxes and spend such a large proportion of the national wealth on welfare, wars and paperwork, they have a huge impact on the economy of the country anyway.

What the government gets up to may seem to be far removed from what marketers do in their day-to-day lives, except of course where legislation prevents us from advertising in a particular way, or selling a particular category of product. In fact, government policy has far-reaching effects on the business environment in which marketers operate. Policy has often shifted according to the current fashionable ideas among economists: whether the ideas are acceptable or not probably depends largely on the prevailing mood of the country. For example, in the Mercantilist era of economic thought, it was assumed that the wealth of a country could be measured by its ownership of precious metals – gold and silver, predominantly. These metals could either be mined or (for countries without mines) be bought using exported products. Thus countries such as England, having no gold mines, were forced to subsidize exports and apply huge tariffs to imports. (Wales does have gold mines, but these are small and have not added appreciably to the country's wealth.) The main effect of raising tariffs on imports was to add considerably to the level of smuggling: the seventeenth-century equivalent of the booze cruise was a short trip to Brittany to bring back French brandy and wines, landing back at an isolated Cornish cove to hide the booty.

A group of French economists, the Physiocrats, did not accept the Mercantilist view of the economy: they believed that agriculture was the true source of all wealth. This view seems to have lasted until the present day in France, but in the eighteenth century it was a new idea. The Physiocrats also believed that income and output formed a circular flow, which could only be disrupted by government interference, so they advocated a laissez-faire attitude. This model turned out to be somewhat simplistic (surprises all round) and of course was not popular with governments, who naturally believe that it is their job to run things.

Smith rejected the idea that agriculture was the only source of wealth, but he did accept the view that governments should stay clear of trying to run the economy. However, a later Classicist, John Stuart Mill (1998 [1848]), pointed out that a laissez-faire attitude might be good for creating wealth, but to ensure its fair distribution governments would need to intervene. Mill's private life was itself a bit laissez-faire: he had a strictly intellectual upbringing, with little room for the emotional side of life, but he certainly made up the lost ground later by having a lengthy affair with his co-author (one Mrs Taylor) while she was married to the unfortunate Mr Taylor. When Mr Taylor died in 1851, Mill married Mrs Taylor and they lived as happily ever after as two economists can. Having discovered girls, so to speak, he became an MP and campaigned for votes for women, as well as writing a book on the subjection of women. The result of this was a large number of baby girls called Emily, Emmeline, Millicent and so forth, presumably so that their grateful mothers could shorten their names to Milly (Mrs Pankhurst, the famous suffragette, was christened Emmeline).

For the purposes of studying marketing, though, it is Mill's contribution to economics that is the most relevant. His view was that wealth could be created very well if government kept well clear, but that the wealth would concentrate in the hands of the few if there were no intervention. So government intervention became acceptable again.

Marxists, of course, called for radical intervention: this culminated in the planned economies of Eastern Europe during the twentieth century, and a fairly even distribution of wealth (nobody had anything). So far we have one vote for laissez-faire and two for intervention.

Next up to bat were the Institutionalists. Institutionalist economists regarded individual economic behaviour as part of a wider social pattern, influenced by current ways of living and modes of thought. They advocated government intervention as a way of ensuring fair distribution of income, adding their voice to Mill's argument that limited intervention to distribute wealth is reasonable, provided it does not interfere with the basic mechanism of creating wealth. On paper this looks fine. In practice it is hard to see how, for example, taxing someone who is currently getting a larger than average share of the wealth will not tend to demotivate that individual from producing even more wealth. Not to mention that taxing so-called 'luxury' goods, such as sports cars and helicopters, has a profound effect on Joe Schmuck, who works on the Lamborghini or Robinson production lines.

Eventually the debate was resolved (temporarily, as it turned out) by an accidental experiment. In the 1930s, the Great Depression proved to be a major problem for governments. Smith had theorized that a rise in unemployment would lead to lower wages and prices, which would in turn stimulate the economy and thus lead to a return to full employment. In fact, the reverse happened. Falling wages meant people could not afford to buy anything, so factories closed and unemployment rose still further. Into the resulting confusion stepped John Maynard Keynes, whose seminal text *The General Theory of Employment, Interest and Money* (Keynes, 1960 [1936]) showed that the government needed to inject money into the economy, and increase spending power to get unemployment down. Keynes was literally a larger-than-life figure: he was 6´ 6˝ tall (two metres, for those who have gone metric) and he ran one of the most successful investment funds of the 1930s on behalf of his college, King's College Cambridge. He was certainly not an ivory-tower academic: he advised the British Government at the Versailles Treaty talks, advised on how to pay for the Second World War, and was instrumental in setting up the Bretton-Woods Agreement on international currency exchanges after the war. He died of a heart attack in 1946, aged 62.

Keynes based his thinking on an adapted version of the Physiocrats' model, in which expenditure, consumption, and production formed a circular flow. In Keynes' model, exports represented an input of wealth into the economy and imports represented an outflow. Likewise, government expenditure represented an input, and taxation represented an outflow. At the time, governments worldwide believed that they needed to balance the budget (that is, take in as much tax as they paid out) in order to maintain the value of the currency against the value of gold, which was an international medium of exchange. Keynes theorized that, as governments took more taxation, unemployment would rise and even more tax would have to be raised from the remaining workers and companies in order to fund government. The theory worked out beautifully, with over 15 per cent of the UK workforce unemployed and even more on short-time working, and (at one point) German industry operating at only 25 per cent of capacity.

Sadly, Keynes was a voice in the wilderness until the Second World War forced the government to spend a lot of money and provide jobs. No one (apart from a few crackpots) would want to have a war just to provide jobs, but the Second World War did kick-start the world economy.

One of the drawbacks of Keynes' theories (as he admitted himself) is that injecting a lot of money into the economy does tend to cause inflation in the long run. 'But in the long run, we're all dead', he is famously quoted as saying. In the 1930s and 1940s, the general feeling was that the problems of (a) unemployment and (b) winning the Second World War were rather more urgent: a theoretical argument about inflation hardly registers on someone who is being bombed nightly by the Luftwaffe, no matter how cogent the argument. After the war, though, successive governments became tempted by the easy vote-winner of injecting non-existent money into the economy in order to create consumer booms, and in the mid-1970s inflation really kicked off. Economists were at a loss to explain what was happening. Most industrial countries had inflation and high unemployment both at the same time – which is supposed by Keynesians to be impossible.

Again a hero appeared, in the unlikely shape of Milton Friedman. An American, Friedman was the founder of the Chicago School of economics, a group of economists who believe in laissez-faire. Friedman (2002 [1962]) advocated (you guessed it) less government interference in the economy, and instead advised governments to control the money supply, allowing it to grow only at the same rate as the economy. Margaret Thatcher in the UK and Ronald Reagan in the USA leaped on this theory, and applied it to their economies, with the result that unemployment tripled – but inflation came down to reasonable levels, and (eventually) employment came back up. Incidentally, in 2005 Friedman also advocated legalizing marijuana – interesting for a guy born in 1912.

What does all this have to do with marketing, you ask? Well, marketers do not operate in a vacuum. They work within an overall business context, and more especially in a national economic context. Whether government is interventionist or not has a profound effect on marketers' ability to sell products and services. The state of the national economy, and the state of the economies of other countries (if one is lucky enough to work for a global organization) affects what consumers do, and consumers (as we know) are the rabbits we are hunting.

small is beautiful – microeconomics

When I was an undergraduate I had two economics lecturers. One was around six feet tall and taught macroeconomics, the other was five feet four and taught microeconomics. Whether physical attributes influence choice of career is debatable, but I have never forgotten that microeconomics is about small economic behaviour.

Microeconomics contributes a lot to marketing thinking because it is concerned with the behaviour of individuals. It does make some key assumptions, which are debatable at the very least, but it is also a real science with numbers and everything, so we should take it seriously.

One of the first assumptions microeconomists make is that consumers are rational and seek to maximize the utility (or usefulness) they can get from their meagre store of money. There are two schools of thought on the utility issue: Cardinalists believe that utility can be measured, and Ordinalists believe that it can't be measured but that people are able to rank different 'baskets' of product and state which would be preferable.

A second assumption is that money has a constant value. If the marginal utility of money changes, for example because someone becomes richer or poorer, this throws the calculations for utility out of synch and we have no idea where we are. In other words, people who have more money than they can spend usefully tend to be a bit more wasteful, whereas those who have recently become poor might be exceptionally careful about what they buy.

Thirdly, microeconomists assume that the utility of each commodity can be measured. The yardstick for measuring utility is money: how much utility can the consumer obtain for a given amount of money? Utility, though, depends on the individual. What is useful to some people is of no value to others, and (more importantly) the utility of a commodity varies at different times even for the same individual.

The fourth assumption is the diminishing value of utility. As the consumer buys more of the product, the usefulness gained by each new addition is reduced. In other words, if you have no shoes at all, a pair of shoes is really useful, but as you buy more pairs their usefulness decreases until, if you have 200 pairs, the shoes are actually becoming a bit of a liability. This is called the axiom of diminishing marginal utility.

Fifthly, we have to assume that the total utility of a basket of goods depends on the quantities of the individual commodities. That is to say, if you have a bag full of groceries, the total value of the groceries is dependent on how much of each one you have (because, after all, the utility decreases as you have more of something).

A consumer is in equilibrium if the marginal utility of a product is equal to its price, because the consumer will be equally happy to save the money or buy the product. If the product's marginal utility is greater than the price, the consumer will buy it, and if the product's marginal utility is less than the price the consumer will not buy it. This has a great deal of logical appeal, and is probably what happens most of the time. Put in simple terms, people like a bargain but do not like to be ripped off. If the product is very cheap, in other words if the marginal utility is much greater than the price, the consumer will keep buying more of the product until the marginal utility is reduced to the point where it is equal to the price (say, 50 pairs of shoes).

As a way of thinking about pricing, this has a certain appeal. As we drop the prices, sales will rise, but only up to a point. After a while cutting prices does not work any more because people have more than enough of the product. Also, the model demonstrates that people are not aware of, or influenced by, the costs of manufacture of a product. They are only influenced by how useful it is to them. Demand would therefore show as a curve on a graph – as price reduces, demand rises but not in a straight line. It will rise at first, but then start declining.

Economists also assume that firms have a role in setting prices – which appears to be common sense, but in the long run it is consumers who decide whether or not they are prepared to pay a particular price, and if they are not so prepared, the price must be cut. Economists make some fairly sweeping assumptions about how firms behave towards pricing, just the same. First, they assume that firms act rationally, as if they were composed of a single individual. This ignores the real decision-making in firms, which is based on office politics, career progression, personal gain, and occasionally some rational concern for the welfare of the firm. Secondly, economists assume that the firm seeks to maximize its profits and that this is the only goal. In many cases, companies are founded for all sorts of reasons – the founder had a whizzo idea that he or she thought ought to be done, or the directors like to make decisions and have fun, or whatever. Also, in recent years boards of directors have been much more concerned with maintaining share value rather than with making profits, since this is actually of more use to shareholders. Thirdly, economists assume that firms are the primary users of factors of production (labour, land, capital and enterprise). They buy these from households, who are assumed to own everything (including the firms themselves).

These assumptions are all somewhat suspect. As a real science, microeconomics has to assume that people are rational, or chaos would be the result, but as anyone who ventures into a city centre on a Saturday night can testify, people sometimes behave irrationally. Economists, of course, are rational, so they tend to have a lot of formulae and deep thinking to do. Secondly, the assumption that utility can be measured objectively is highly unlikely – whether a product is useful or not depends on the individual, the time, the place, and the circumstances. A useless old piece of rope might be thrown out of a garage during a clear-out, but the same piece of rope might be extremely useful as a tow-rope for a broken-down car on a wet night.

Regarding the assumptions economists make about firms, these are also highly suspect. Firms do not act any more rationally than the individuals who work for them. This may be extremely rational, it may be entirely capricious, or it may be somewhere in between. Secondly, many firms do not seek to maximize profits, and there are many organizations which are non-profit-making but which still sell and buy. Thirdly, we have to perform some fairly clever mental gymnastics to account for factor purchases by other organizations (such as the government) which do not produce anything which is sold. We have to start assuming that the government charges taxes for its outputs, and that consumers have choice about paying taxes, for example. There is some truth in this, incidentally: a government which raises taxes beyond the point at which people are prepared to pay finds either that it is voted out of office, or (as the Labour Government of the 1970s found) people simply switch to a cash economy in which they do not declare their true incomes. Even in the early 2000s, many people avoid the high taxes on wines, spirits and tobacco simply by buying these products abroad.

Interestingly, economists do not assume that governments act rationally and consistently. Inter-departmental conflict is often used to explain theories about government intervention in the economy. Whether this is a reflection on governments or on economists will be left as an exercise for the student.

A great deal of microeconomics is based around the concept of a basket of goods. The theory is that if you confront an individual with two shopping baskets with a different mix of goods in each, but to the same monetary value, the individual would be able to say which basket he or she prefers. Economists assume (for the sake of argument) that the individual in question would always choose the same basket. Also, the assumption is that adding more baskets will still lead to consistency – that if someone prefers Basket A over Basket B, and Basket C over Basket A, then Basket C will be the overall preference (you might want to read that again – I just had to).

This idea of comparing baskets leads us neatly on to the concept of the indifference curve. An indifference curve is the locus of points which yield the same utility. This means that the curve is drawn along a line of points where the individual sees the baskets of goods as being of equal value – he or she is indifferent as to which one to buy, because they are worth the same. In the simplest case, with only two products in the basket, the consumer will be happy to substitute one for another up to a point.

Here's an example. Imagine you are in the pub with some friends, and you send the idiot friend to the bar to buy some beer and sandwiches. Because the bar is busy, you decide to stock up a bit and order some extra beers. You ask your friend to bring three pints of beer and two packs of sandwiches, and your other friend (the greedy one) asks for one pint of beer and four packs of sandwiches. The idiot comes back with two pints for you and three packs of sandwiches, and four pints for your greedy friend and only one pack of sandwiches.

In those circumstances, you might feel indifferent about the mistake: you can take a pack of sandwiches home, and being one pint short isn't exactly going to spoil your day. Equally, your fat friend might accept the situation. Of course, you could always do a swap – if you swap your sandwiches for his beer, you would both be better off because you would now have exactly what you wanted in the first place.

This principle can be extended further, of course. For your greedy friend to be happy with no sandwiches at all, he would have to have a lot more than just one more pint of beer; and for you to be happy with no beer at all, you would have had to have a lot of sandwiches. In those circumstances, an exchange would leave both of you better off in terms of both beer and sandwiches.

This principle was first explained by a gentleman who rejoiced in the name Francis Ysidro Edgeworth. Edgeworth's name came about because his father, while a student, decided to elope with a penniless Catalonian refugee whom he met on the steps of the British Museum while he was supposed to be on his way to Germany. Francis Ysidro was actually born in Ireland, in (wait for it) Edgeworthstown, a place which he eventually inherited. He was a life-long bachelor, despite courting Beatrix Potter, so had no one to leave the town to. What he did leave, however, was a clear model to explain trade (Edgeworth, 1881). It was refined into a box-shaped diagram by Vilfredo Federico Damaso Pareto in 1906 (a busy year for Pareto – he also gave us the 80/20 rule in that year). The Edgeworth Box explains how trade always makes us better off.

This is another of those concepts which is obvious when someone explains it. Trade makes us better off because otherwise people wouldn't do it. The pub landlord wants your money more than he wants the beer – he has plenty of beer, more than he could ever drink by himself, but he needs the money to pay his overheads. You, on the other hand, clearly want the beer more than you want the money, or you wouldn't do the exchange.

Since marketing is largely concerned with managing exchange, Edgeworth and Pareto have made an important contribution to marketing thought. Now we know that we can offer people bundles of benefits (products) and we can vary the bundles to make them more or less attractive to specific people. If the bundle is more attractive than the money, people will buy the product: we can safely assume that, as people get richer, their supply of money approaches the point at which keeping it becomes less attractive than spending it and we can sell them stuff. The more money someone has, the less valuable it seems in comparison with bundles of benefits (helicopters, Porsches, and so forth).

Because people make comparisons between different bundles of benefits, and are prepared to accept substitutions, it may be difficult to predict demand. In effect, marketers are competing with every other 'bundle of benefits' for the consumer's hard-earned money. However, we can say with some confidence that the demand curve for most goods rises as prices fall – people are inclined to buy more of something if they can get it cheaper.

In some cases people would have been prepared to pay a lot more for the goods than is actually being asked. In other words, the consumer picked up a bargain. Alfred Marshall (see above) first pointed this out, so it has become known as the Marshallian surplus (Marshall, 1997 [1890]). For marketers, the key to success lies in understanding where the cut-off point lies. In an ideal world, we want consumers to go away feeling they had a bargain, but we want to push the price as high as we can in order to maximize our own profits. To do this, it would help if we knew how price-sensitive consumers were. In other words, what is the slope of the demand curve. If the curve slopes sharply, a large change in price would be needed to make a small change in demand. If the curve slopes gradually, a small change in price would lead to a large change in demand. This is called price elasticity of demand.

The elasticity concept says that some products are hardly price-sensitive at all – salt is the usual example, because it's a very cheap commodity which is not bought very often, so most people wouldn't even know what it costs, let alone spend time shopping around for a bargain. On the other hand, cars seem to be much more price-sensitive: even a relatively small change in price affects demand fairly strongly, at least in the kind of cars I buy. Elasticity depends in part on the existence of close substitutes, so perhaps a price rise for Nissan means that more customers switch to Ford, or vice versa.

Elasticity of demand also applies to income – as income rises, so does demand. An interesting side issue here is the concept of necessity and luxury. A good which is an absolute necessity would, one assumes, have a completely inelastic demand curve.

If you can't survive without it, you'd pay any price for it, would you not? In practice, no such item exists, and in fact some items which are necessary for life (water, for instance) are so cheap we can flush toilets with it. This means that the distinction between luxuries and necessities is an artificial one at best.

Finally, demand may be affected by related products. This is a useful thing to know because sales of one product may be a useful predictor for sales of another product. There was a time when sales of wedding rings was a good predictor for sales of baby clothes, with about a one-year time delay: those days are gone. Sales of cars precede sales of spare parts such as tyres and headlight bulbs, though, and we know that at Christmas sales of turkey and plum pudding precede sales of diet books. Such products are called complements, because their demand curves are complemented by the demand curves for other products. Likewise there are products which are regarded as substitutes: if there is a sharp rise in the cost of potatoes, for example, sales of rice or pasta are likely to rise as people switch to the nearest alternatives. Economists also consider the effect of wealth reduction: if the cost of mortgages rises (due to a rise in interest rates) the remaining cash within the household will be correspondingly less, so the family will have to spend less on other things. This is a familiar situation for most homeowners, which is why most people dream of paying off their mortgages.

Economists also talk about markets, and have a particular view of what constitutes a market. The economists' definition of a market is 'an area over which buyers and sellers negotiate the exchange of a well-defined commodity'. Markets are separated from each other by the type of commodity sold, by natural economic barriers such as transport costs, and by barriers created by governments (for example, high customs duties on some goods). Economists accept that markets are interlinked: all commodities compete for consumers' income (this is the concept of the economic choice), and also that costs of transportation or high customs duties might not separate the markets if the basic cost of the commodity is sufficiently cheaper in one market than in another. This kind of thinking is very much in line with marketing thinking – we assume that consumers only have a limited amount of money to spend, and that therefore we are competing with other firms whose products provide similar benefits.

Economists also assert that different markets differ from each other according to the degree of competitiveness shown by the various buyers and sellers involved in the market. Thus they account for a degree of human variation – although most economic theories centre around markets which are large enough that no single buyer or seller has sufficient power to influence price, which is a ridiculous concept since there is almost always one major firm in the market which is able to control what goes on.

Markets can themselves have an overall demand curve, which is affected mainly by macroeconomic factors (see above), such as interest rate rises, unemployment levels, international competition, and so forth. Demand curves can shift sideways – the same shape of curve can be moved by an overall shift in demand due to environmental factors, by sudden increases or decreases in supply, or sudden increases and decreases in demand. Note that economists also have a lot of theories about the supply side of the equation – these are of interest to marketers in terms of our responses to competition, and the possibility of an over-supply which would drive prices down. On the other hand, marketers always seek to differentiate their products from those of the competition, so they tend to regard other products as being an indirect threat.

A final word on markets from economists. They distinguish between a free market (one in which production is in the market sector and is not controlled by government) and a command economy, or centrally-controlled economy, in which all production and consumption is controlled by the central authorities, that is the government. In fact, there has never been a pure example of either type, although the Bolsheviks in Russia during the 1920s came close to having a controlled economy (issuing decrees about prices and forcing people to work in various occupations, and even instituting a slave economy under the doubtful logic of saying that slavery run by capitalists was exploitation, but slavery under socialism was self-organization by the proletariat. One imagines that the average Russian serf would find it difficult to see the difference – but that's the drawback of being uneducated). For economists, a suitable aggregation of markets is called an economy (for example, the UK economy, the European economy). Whether an economy is a command economy or a free-market economy is only a question of degree – the former Communist countries, which were theoretically command economies, had considerable scope for free enterprise, and the so-called free-market economies of Western Europe actually have a substantial proportion of government-owned enterprises within their borders.

So where are we with the microeconomists? Have they helped us understand people any better? In some ways they have. Provided consumers are rational, thoughtful beings who go about their consumption activities in a logical and ordered fashion, the economists can explain what they do and why they do it. Provided the models consider simple cases (one or two consumers, a few product categories, some shopping baskets and a stopwatch and most microeconomists are as happy as sandboys), they hold up fairly well to scrutiny. But what happens when people are influenced by the wicked marketers, or by their friends, or by the influence of alcohol? How do they cope then?

For these explanations we need to look at the contribution made by behavioural scientists. This is the basis of the next chapter. Meanwhile, perhaps we should consider whether economics is a real science or not. Does it have boundaries? Does it have a clear core subject which it is intended to investigate? Does it carry out investigations which other researchers can duplicate? Does it seek to discover rules which can be universally applied? Does it deal with the abstract rather than with the concrete? I think the answers to these questions are mainly Yes, which (at least by my definition) makes economics a real science. As an underpinning for marketing thought, economics makes a very good beginning – it does not come anywhere near to explaining the whole picture, however.

2

Behavioural Scientists

Because people are not rational, marketers look beyond basic 'economics' theories of consumption and demand, and consider contributions from people who study behaviour. Behavioural scientists are psychologists, sociologists, and anthropologists of various types: there are cross-over disciplines such as social psychology, but broadly people tend to slot themselves into one or other of the main three categories. Each group has contributed something to our understanding of what makes people buy things, and in particular each group has contributed something about the less rational motives for people's behaviour. Each discipline has also contributed quite a lot to our understanding of people who sell things, too – much of what we know about managing the salesforce comes from the behavioural sciences.

Psychology is the study of thought processes. It concentrates mainly on the individual therefore – although some of the experiments conducted at Duke University by Dr Joseph Banks Rhine in the 1930s and 1940s indicated that some people can share their thoughts with others via telepathy, this would properly come under the heading of parapsychology. The Greek word *para* means almost, or slightly less than but nearly, so parapsychology is presumably slightly less than but nearly psychology.

Sociology is the study of behaviour in groups. Humans beings are herd animals: in prehistoric times we had to co-operate in order to survive, and the habit has persisted. In 20,000 BC anybody who did not get on well with the other tribe members, behaving like them and looking like them, was liable to be left for the bears: in AD 2000 anybody who does not get on with the tribe is demonstrably a nerd and is left out of all the fun. This means that people's behaviour is very dependent on what they think the group wants them to do – whether it involves rubbing woad into one's navel, or buying Nike trainers, we are driven by other people's opinions.

Anthropology is the study of what makes us human. It includes archaeology (the study of ancient civilizations and cultures) as well as cultural anthropology (which is the study of culture). Anthropologists want to know why the group thinks it's a good idea to rub woad in their navels in the first place. Anthropologists often spend a lot of time living with people from different cultures: the cliché of the anthropologist living deep in the jungle with a tribe of cannibals is not far from the truth, although the luckier (or perhaps brighter) anthropologists choose to live with lobster fishing communities in Brittany.

Behavioural scientists sometimes look at consumer behaviour directly, but in most cases they simply offer the theories that marketers then pick up and seize as their own. Consumer behaviour journals are therefore almost always filled with articles by marketers rather than articles by full-on psychologists. Equally, not many marketers seem to read articles in psychology journals or sociology journals, judging by the references I see at the ends of journal papers. This is perhaps something we should think about a bit more.

psychology: thinking about thought

Psychology goes back a long way, in fact probably to the first time people began to become self-aware and to realize that something happens in the brain which is independent of physical needs and immediate problems. Aristotle wrote about psychology (*psyche* being Greek for 'the soul'), and Galen (the Roman doctor) described the structure of the brain in about AD 170. Later, in AD 1020 an individual called Avocenna suggested that the three ventricles of the brain described by Galen performed five separate cognitive functions: common sense, imagination, cogitation, estimation and memory. How Avocenna arrived at this profound conclusion remains hidden in the mists of time, but we know that the Romans understood enough about the brain to be able to perform surgery on it, as did some even earlier civilizations.

During the early nineteenth century, there was a widespread belief that the shape of the brain determined the shape of thought, and much effort was expended on the study of phrenology. Phrenology is the study of the shape of the head, from which it was supposed that mental characteristics could be deduced. (This belief has persisted in a somewhat diluted form into modern times – even thirty years ago people would say 'You want your bumps felt', if they thought someone was acting crazy or stupid.) In general, phrenology is now regarded as rubbish, but some of its basic tenets turned out to be true. For example, phrenologists believed that use of a particular part of the brain more than another would result in it becoming larger, rather as muscles do: a study of London taxi drivers published in 1997 shows that their right hippocampus was enlarged as a result of remembering complex routes around the city (Maguire et al., 1997).

Apart from a few interesting aspects such as this, though, it turns out that the shape of your head has very little, if anything, to do with what goes on inside it. Phrenology therefore gave way to psychology proper. Probably the first psychologist that most people have heard of would be Sigmund Freud. Freud believed that the psyche is divided into three sections: the id (which is the part of the brain devoted to basic impulses and wicked desires), the ego (which is the conscious part of the brain where you do most of your thinking), and the superego (which is your conscience, devoted to making you behave yourself). The id operates below the conscious level, as does a large part of the superego, so thought processes (the mind) are further divided into conscious and subconscious.

This analysis is very appealing. The id is a totally selfish entity: it is demanding and whining, like a two-year-old, but it has overtones of laddishness which would shame a Club 18–30 holiday-maker. The superego is all sweetness and light, like Mary Poppins but with a somewhat 'schoolmistress' attitude to your behaviour: it is, in fact, your conscience, and Freud thought of it as an internalized parent. Between the two lies the ego, trying to pacify the id without upsetting the superego, rather like a marriage guidance counsellor trying to organize a compromise between two people who would otherwise be heading for the divorce courts. Freud believed that schizophrenia (split personality – not dual personality) was caused by a person's inability to make a permanent settlement between the id and the superego, so that continual tension exists in the person's head. This results in violent mood swings as one or the other subconscious element tries to take over. (Despite all those jokes you've heard, this is not the same as a multiple personality. Multiple personalities are different people inhabiting the same body – schizophrenics know exactly who they are all the time, but they have difficulty controlling their actions.)

Freud's main interest was in curing mental illness. He came to the lunatic business when the standard treatment for mental disorders was to lock people up and throw away the key, while subjecting them to 'treatments' which look more like torture to the modern eye. Freud is responsible for the belief that madness (or mental illness, rather) can be treated by psychotherapy, specifically psychoanalysis, in which people are asked to talk about their childhoods, their relationships with their parents (since the superego is an internalized parent) and their sexual attitudes and preferences. Freud is also responsible for the folk-belief that all psychiatrists speak with Austrian accents and ask the patients to 'lie on the couch and tell me about your childhood'.

Like many psychiatrists since, Freud's initial interest in the mind probably resulted from his own mental illnesses. He suffered from occasional depression, and used cocaine to treat it (unremarkable in the nineteenth century, but not something one would recommend in the twenty-first). He almost became famous for his work on the analgesic effects of cocaine, but was beaten to the publishing stage by an old friend and colleague, Carl Koller, who is now credited with the work. Freud was diverted away from this work altogether following the death of a close friend from a dual addiction to both morphine and cocaine.

From a marketer's viewpoint, Freudian psychology has much to offer. We can appeal to the id (and often do) along the lines of: 'Go on – you deserve a treat!' Or to the superego: 'Please give generously. A few pounds from you can make all the difference to some of the world's poorest people.' Or to the ego: 'You can save pounds on your heating bills next winter by insulating your house.' Appeals to the id strengthen the id's case when negotiating with the ego; appeals to the superego likewise. These appeals are largely emotional, whereas appeals to the ego are rational.

After Freud, psychology took off rapidly as a science. Different branches of psychology emerged, each looking at thought processes from a slightly different angle: cognitive psychologists consider the thought processes themselves; behavioural psychologists analyse thought processes by examining the behaviours they produce; neuroscience considers thought processes in terms of the physical activities within the brain, and so forth. The upshot of all this activity is a very detailed view of how people think, which is of course very useful to marketers.

Three of the key marketing issues which marketing academics have pinched from psychology are motivation, perception, and attitude formation and change.

motivation: driving people on

Motivation is what results when the actual state of the individual differs from the desired state. If your actual state is poor and hungry, and your desired state is rich and well-fed, you might become motivated to go out and get a job (or go and rob somebody outside a restaurant). Motivation has a specific direction: the actual hunger or poverty creates a drive, which is the force involved, but the decision to rob or job is what creates the motivation.

Marketers would really love to know exactly what motivates people to buy one item rather than another, but the mechanisms for finding out are still somewhat primitive. Asking people is not always a good guide – we might ask someone why he is attending a religious revival and be told 'Because my brother was born in October'. Hmmm … How's that again? 'My brother was born in October but I was born in December, so I always got a combined Christmas and birthday present, but he got two presents. That made me jealous, and I really hated my brother and we gradually drifted apart. Then I heard that he was taken seriously ill, and I thought I should go to see him to patch things up and apologise for being so stupid, and on the way I had a car accident and ended up in hospital. While I was in hospital I met the hospital chaplain, and I was complaining to him that my brother, who had by now recovered, had not been to see me even though I only had the accident because I was trying to make up the differences between us. The chaplain made me see that it was my own selfishness and greed that had caused the rift in the first place, and that God had punished me for my sins. I don't think God should punish people when they are trying to put things right, so I have come to this religious revival with a gun and I am going to shoot the preacher.'

Which goes to show that motivations can be complex.

Marketers spend a considerable amount of effort in encouraging people to see that their actual state is not really very good at all. We can't do much about the actual state in any absolute sense, but we can try to make people dissatisfied with it by making it seem undesirable, thus creating a new desired state. The bigger the gap between the actual and desired states, the bigger the motivation to do something about it, so we try to make that gap as big as possible by showing people what a beautiful place the desired state is.

So far so good. I have no way of proving this, but I suspect that about two-thirds of marketing communication is directed at activating needs by making people dissatisfied with their actual state. The remaining budget is spent on directing them to specific brands. This is the Dark Side of the Force: it is the manipulative bit. The Good Side of the Force is that marketers also spend a lot of effort on devising products which will fill the gap between the actual and desired states as fully as possible: the better the fit, the more likely the product is to sell in large quantities. This means that marketers have a somewhat ambiguous, nay contradictory, role as far as motivation goes. On the one hand, we try to set up as motivational a situation as we possibly can, then on the other hand we try to take the motivation back to zero, for a price. This does not sit well with the idea of customer centrality.

There have been a number of theories of motivation. Perhaps the most famous is Maslow's Hierarchy of Needs (which is described more fully in Chapter 4), but other researchers have come up with other ideas. Two notable examples are Herzberg's Dual Factor Theory (Herzberg, 1966), and Vroom's Expectancy Theory (Vroom, 1964).

Fred Herzberg was a medical researcher who looked at motivation in the workplace. Essentially, he found that motivation comes in two basic colours: hygiene factors and motivators. Hygiene factors are those elements which one would expect as a matter of course: for example, one expects a car to have a windscreen (although there was a time when windscreens were an optional extra). Motivators are the extras which create a greater motivation, or (in the workplace) a more vigorous activity level.

The basic concept is nicely generalizable to marketing. Customers expect certain minimum features in the product (nowadays one would be surprised to find a car without a radio, for instance). There is a slight problem in that the goalposts keep being moved – people expect more and more as standard, so it becomes harder to find a motivator: it is only a matter of time before people expect cars to come equipped with microwave ovens for those on-the-road snacks. Herzberg was criticized at the time he published his work because he found that salaries are hygiene factors not motivators, and there was some scepticism about this, but in a way it makes sense. After all, if we were all motivated entirely by money, we would all be drug dealers and porn stars, because that's where the money is (see Chapter 1).

As an aside, Herzberg used the term 'hygiene' because he was a medical researcher. Those were the factors he thought were necessary to prevent the 'disease' of demotivation. Prior to Herzberg, people had tended to think of work as being simply an unpleasant necessity – it was Herzberg who demonstrated that work itself is fulfilling and interesting.

Vroom's Expectancy Theory says that motivation depends on three factors: expectancy, which is the degree to which the person feels that the proposed action can be carried out effectively;

instrumentality, which is the degree to which the individual believes that the proposed action will lead to a reward; and valence, which is the value placed on the reward being offered. Expectancy theory is used a lot in workplace motivation, especially with salespeople, so it is useful in marketing management. When motivating consumers, it is useful in thinking through sales promotions or loyalty schemes: if someone does not believe that they can accumulate a reasonable number of frequent-flyer miles, they are liable not to participate in a frequent flyer scheme at all, for example.

These views of motivation are not mutually exclusive. We can pick about between them, and even combine them, and try to get a clearer view of what motivates people, but at the end of the day motivation is a complex area. Most people are rationalizing rather than rational – they act first, and justify their decisions afterwards. Our reasons for behaving as we do are often obscure even to ourselves, never mind psychological researchers.

perception: creating a view of the world

We live in a complex world. It contains too many surprises for a hairless ape, and we are remarkably easy to kill compared with other animals. Understanding how the world works is what keeps us alive, so we spend a lot of our time learning about the world and figuring it out. This is perception in action.

Perception is one of the most important areas for marketers. Perception is about the ways people develop an understanding of the world around them by processing information gleaned through the senses. It is a process both of synthesis and of analysis: people reject most of the stimuli that they receive, only really taking in information of direct interest. At the same time, this leaves gaps in people's knowledge which needs to be filled in by inventing information. Thus each of us has a somewhat different understanding of how the world is made up, and what the rules are. Luckily we have close-enough world views so that we can work well together, at least we do if our experiences have been broadly similar – naturally, if we were to meet up with someone from a radically different cultural background, the situation might be different. For practical, day-to-day purposes we can get along fine, though: differences in perception simply give us a chance to have interesting conversation and/or arguments.

Anchoring our perceptions to something we can all agree on is a useful device which prevents us from straying too far. In the 1970s James Gibson put forward the theory of affordances (Gibson, 1977). Affordances are the fixed points from which perception is defined. Gibson based the theory on work done with pilot training in the Second World War: it became clear that pilots take their cues from fixed objects (such as the horizon or the sun) rather than directly from their kinaesthetic senses. This is essential for a pilot, because the aeroplane moves around: as an aircraft turns, the downward pressure on the pilot stays straight down through the seat, so without looking at the horizon there is no sensation of turning. In a similar way, members of the same culture have similar perceptual reference points which they use as anchors to each other and to their perceptions.

One of the problems about discussing perception is that the word has entered the general language as meaning 'wrong'. People often say, 'That's just your perception', when they mean 'You've had the wool pulled over your eyes'. In fact, perception *is* reality – the only reality we have is the perceptual map in our heads. Scary stuff, especially when we know that other people (including those rascally marketers) are trying to shift our perceptions around. In practice, moving people's perception of the world is not easy. For one thing, everything we take in is interpreted in the light of what we already know (psychologists call this the law of primacy). Secondly, we are usually fairly comfortable with our world view – after all, it has worked fairly well so far. Thirdly, there is a natural suspicion about being manipulated: we resist being influenced by other people unless we have specifically requested some information.

This does not prevent marketers from giving it their best shot, however. When marketers talk of repositioning products, they are talking about moving the product somewhere else in the consumers' perceptual maps. Changing the map by which someone navigates through their world is serious stuff, even when the change is relatively minor: it might not be a big deal if the product is unimportant to the individual, but it could be serious if the product is one in which the individual places great store.

This leads us neatly on to attitudes and attitude change.

attitudes: dealing with the world as we see it

An attitude is a learned predisposition to respond in a specific way to a specific stimulus: it may be positive or negative, it may or may not involve action, but an attitude is a useful 'shorthand' way of making decisions. Attitudes give us a set of prepared responses, so we don't have to think too much: decision rules (heuristics) usually derive from attitudes.

People form attitudes about most things, from brussels sprouts to marriage partners, and often the attitudes last for a very long time. Such attitudes are stable, so the first move in changing an attitude is to destabilize it. Usually this is done by introducing new information, or by introducing a new feeling about the attitudinal object. This way of viewing attitude change was first described by Petty and Cacioppo (1983). They called the 'information' route the direct route, and the 'emotional' route is called the peripheral route. There is a connotation here to suggest that the peripheral route is somehow not quite fair: not being direct, it may be somehow a little shady. This contributes to the view that marketers are manipulative, and can make people do things they otherwise would not do. The ability to do this is the Holy Grail for marketers: if only we could push the right buttons, we would not have to bother producing things people actually want to buy!

These routes to attitude change work (when they do work, at any rate) because attitudes are believed to be composed of three elements: cognition (what we think about the attitudinal object), affect (what we feel about the attitudinal object) and conation (what we intend to do about it). Conation is the odd one out because it is *intended* behaviour, not *actual* behaviour. For example, you might have an intense dislike for someone, expressed as follows: 'He borrowed fifty quid off me and never paid it back [cognition]. I hate people who do that [affect]. I'm going to punch his teeth in.' The final part of this attitude may or may not happen, especially if new information comes to light (for example, you find out he's been taking boxing lessons, and is getting on rather well with them).

Attitude change is clearly of great interest to marketers (as it is to most people). If people have a negative attitude towards what we offer, they are unlikely to make the exchanges we would like: if their attitude is positive towards a competitor's products, we would like them to be a little less positive towards the competitors, and a little more positive towards us. In short, we want to be loved. In practice, attitudes are often difficult to change once they become established. Destabilizing an attitude by introducing new information or by creating a new emotional element is often doomed to failure because the individual concerned simply rejects the new information. Hurrah for independence of thought.

This illustrates an interesting point, often missed by those who belong to the 'marketing is evil and must die' school. The point is that consumers (i.e., people) are not as stupid as some people would have us believe. They are quite capable of making judgements, particularly about information being received from marketers. This is because people have had a lot of practice in resisting persuasion – most communications between people have some element of persuasion in them. We therefore respond well to communications and offers which we think are of benefit, and reject those which we think are not. Rejecting the information is, however, the easiest option because it avoids having to reformulate the decision rules that stemmed from the attitude in the first place. In other words, accepting the new information leads to cognitive dissonance. Cognitive dissonance is the internal stress set up by trying to hold two different opinions at once: it is often resolved by changing one's attitude.

In 1959, two researchers called Leon Festinger and J. Merrill Carlsmith played a cruel trick on their students (as many lecturers do). They recruited students for an 'experiment' in which the students were required to perform a tedious task (specifically, putting pegs into holes in a board, turning the pegs a quarter-turn, then removing the pegs). After doing this until boredom had set in, they were told that the experiment was over, but they were asked to assist in recruiting more students. To do this, they were asked if they could tell the new recruit (who was actually in on the joke) that the task was really interesting and good fun. In other words, they were asked to lie through their teeth. Some of the students were paid $1 for their help in recruiting the new student, others were paid $20, and a control group were not paid anything (Festinger and Carlsmith, 1959).

In 1959 $20 was a substantial some of money. It would be about $600 in today's money, so one would imagine that these students would have been very slick in lying to their fellow-student. Not so. The researchers found that the students who were paid $1 became much more animated and persuasive than the ones who were paid $20. The theory is that the students who were paid less could not justify telling lies on the grounds of being paid, so they actually had to believe the lies. The better-paid students could justify the lies more easily – after all, they were being well-paid to lie.

The idea that an attitude change can be developed more easily by offering a *low* incentive is an interesting one. It seems to imply that over-generous sales promotions may be counter-productive as well as expensive, and also implies that salespeople might be more motivated by (say) a company tie than by a generous bonus. In fact both these circumstances have been observed in the wild, so perhaps Festinger and Carlsmith were on to something after all.

An interesting side discussion – Festinger and Carlsmith's experiment would almost certainly not be allowed to go ahead nowadays. University ethics committees take a dim view of any research where the subjects of the research do not know what is really going on. Since the same is true of many of the psychological experiments carried out in the past, one wonders whether research is being stifled by ethics committees.

The other great event of 1959 was that my mother told me that I was going to have a new little sister. This turned out to be untrue – my brother was born in 1960, and turned out to be a real little hooligan who destroyed everything I owned. Henry, if you're reading this, don't think I've forgotten.

This leads us on to consider the role of groups, of which family is undoubtedly the most important.

'I wouldn't join any club that would accept a person like me as a member'

Groucho Marx's comment on group membership probably has resonances for many people. We are all members of groups, some of which we would rather not be members of. Sociology is the study of behaviour in groups, and behaviour of groups.

Sociology is a relatively recent science. Serious study of social groups only started with Emile Durkheim in the late nineteenth century, although some study of groups had been part of the remit of philosophers and writers such as Thomas Hobbes, medical writers such as John Gaunt, and political philosophers such as John Locke. Durkheim believed that society had a life of its own, separate from that of its members; that group behaviour, in effect, was not merely the sum of the behaviours of members of the group, but was a special type of collective behaviour. The second belief that Durkheim espoused was that the members of a group will tend to perpetuate the existence and stability of the group. This is an interesting concept: Durkheim seems to be saying that groups protect themselves, and that a group can only be changed by outside influence. It also means that individuals might well sacrifice themselves for the good of the group – and we even regard such sacrifices as laudable. The classic example is Kamikaze pilots: they were prepared to crash their aircraft into enemy ships in order to help the national war effort, and consequently were regarded as heroes. At a more mundane level, people who are prepared to go out of their way to help a friend are regarded as good people: people who only ever do things for their own benefit are regarded as selfish, bad people.

This relates strongly to the point made by Marx (Groucho, not Karl). Someone who is selfish would not want to join a club comprised of other selfish people, because the opportunities for advancing one's own position are limited in those circumstances.

Durkheim also wrote a book about suicide, in which he suggested that suicide could come about because the person feels like an outsider, and suffers from what Durkheim called anomie. Alternatively, suicide could come about because the person is extremely well-connected with the group and is prepared to make the supreme sacrifice for the group's welfare. In the example of Japanese kamikaze pilots the latter was the case: it was not that they were eager to die, but rather that they were prepared to die in order to protect their homeland. The fact that most of them were romantic teenagers who probably didn't actually believe that they were going to die permanently probably helped the recruitment drive as well.

As marketers we do not expect our customers to kill themselves if they do not buy the product (although some marketers might like the idea). However, marketers are aware that people can be driven to desperate extremes in order to protect a group, join a group, or remain part of a group. Also, group behaviour does often seem to take on a life of its own: this is often used in advertising which shows groups of people having a good time (usually by sharing the soft drink, beer or whatever the product happens to be).

Durkheim also considered the effect of division of labour, but unlike Adam Smith (see Chapter 1), Durkheim considered the effects it would have on people's behaviour in groups. He saw division of labour as being a unifying factor, developing communities of mutually-dependant people who would feel included or excluded according to the way the work was divided between them. Durkheim believed that the rules for living embodied in these groups are passed on through the group and through the generations by a process of learning called socialization. Socialization is the gradual moulding of the person's behaviour by comparison with the group.

This process of comparing one's own behaviour with that of the group is a key issue in sociology, and also in marketing. Marketers frequently use actors to model the use of the products in group situations, showing how the person who uses the product can become popular with a desirable group of people. The type of group can vary considerably, of course: some groups are more important and influential than others, some are more desirable than others, and some groups (the so-called automatic groups) are groups which we belong to whether we want to or not (our racial group, for example, or our gender, short of major surgery). An interesting problem for advertising creatives is that the model in the advert has to be (a) like the target consumers, so that they relate to the situation, and (b) attractive, so that the consumers watch the advert. These two aims may be difficult to reconcile, or would be if it were not for the magical effect of perception, by which we perceive ourselves as we wish we were rather than as we actually are.

One of the most interesting aspects of sociology, for me, was the revelation that all organizations are segmental in nature. In other words, they only take and use a small segment of the personalities of each of their members. This means that each of us presents a different face to each of the groups we are involved with, which is probably just as well. After all, one would not behave the same way in church as one does in the pub, and our behaviour with our friends is usually very different from our behaviour with our parents. This being the case, we often feel uneasy when we are in the company of people from different groups: meeting someone from work when we are out for the evening, or (worse) meeting an elderly relative when we are on the way home from a night out ....

Because we play different roles in different situations, you may get the idea that people are two-faced (multifaceted sounds better, but it means the same thing). Who is the real person, if we are all acting out roles? Erving Goffman tried to explain this in his book *The Presentation of Self in Everyday Life* which was published in 1959 (the same year as Festinger and Carlsmith's experiment with the students). Goffman suggested that we are all, in fact, actors, and therefore we use props, script, costume, and actions to present the roles we play. We have a stage on which we perform for the audience, and a backstage area where we are 'ourselves' with our closest friends and lovers (Goffman, 1959). The dramaturgical analogy, as it is called, is not entirely a Goffman invention, of course: Shakespeare said 'All the world's a stage, and all the men and women merely players' but he said it 350 years earlier.

This interesting aspect of human nature accounts for a lot of flamboyant behaviour, as well as a need for an extensive wardrobe. Most of us have work clothes, 'going-out' clothes, holiday clothes, and slobbing-out clothes, and some people have even more categories or sub-categories of clothes, depending on what kind of going-out they are indulging in, and what kind of holiday they are planning. We also need props – cigarettes, wine glasses, shooting-sticks, briefcases, laptops, fast cars, the latest gadgets, anything we can show off to our friends with. We also need the right friends, co-stars who can be relied upon to deliver the right lines at the right time, or who look the part, or who enhance our own reputations. We spend a great deal of time and effort on setting the stage: decorating our houses, personalizing our working spaces, having the right location and décor for our hobbies (what flying-club would be complete without a propeller on the wall?) and even choosing the location for a specific performance. How often do people say, 'This isn't the right place for this conversation. Let's meet up later at the pub/the office/my house/ the magistrate's court.'

It is not exactly rocket science to see where marketers have an input into life as theatre. Selling props, providing venues, providing the set, the costumes, and even some of the dialogue are all activities marketers can undertake profitably. The only thing marketers don't do is sell tickets – but watch this space!

anthropology – studying culture

The word 'anthropology' derives from the Greek word for man (*andhros*) and of course the word for study (*logos*). Anthropology is sometimes defined as 'the study of human beings and whatever helps explain their existence and behaviour' (Hicks and Gwynne, 1996). This seems to be a somewhat broad definition, encompassing virtually everything in the world, so anthropologists traditionally subdivide their studies into biological anthropology (which is about the physical aspects of being human), archaeology (focusing on the material remains of people of the past), anthropological linguistics (the study of the development of languages) and cultural anthropology (the study of culture).

For marketers, biological anthropology has only a few areas of interest. It tends to look at how people became human, so biological anthropologists spend a lot of time observing the other great apes, or investigating extinct sub-species of humanity. Not much help in terms of selling washing-powder.

Likewise, archaeology only offers a few usable concepts, although of course some products use imagery based on people or objects from the distant past: when Tutankhamen's tomb was discovered by Howard Carter in the 1920s it sparked a wave of interest in anything Egyptian, from clothing to jewellery. Such events are relatively rare.

Anthropological linguistics is an interesting area since marketers are, perhaps above anything else, communicators. Anthropologists can show us how languages evolve, and can also provide us with vocabularies for new slang, sources of terms in common use, and so forth. In most cases marketers are likely to simply write first and ask questions afterwards, though.

Therefore cultural anthropology is the branch that provides us with the most basic theory. Culture is the set of shared beliefs and behaviours that a particular society passes on through the generations. Culture includes language, customs, religious and other beliefs, and group attitudes and behaviours. When studying, anthropologists often immerse themselves in a culture for long periods – in order to understand the culture fully, they need to become almost part of it. Anthropology may be the least understood of the social sciences by the average lay person.

For one thing, anthropology tends to be associated with studies of 'primitive' tribes who live deep in the jungles and deserts of the world. The blame for this misconception might be placed with anthropologists such as Margaret Mead, who spent a great deal of time studying tribes in Samoa, New Guinea and Indonesia, and who enjoyed putting cats among pigeons. Mead discovered (for example) that gender roles are learned, not determined by biology – a revolutionary idea in the 1920s when her work was published. She had a somewhat unorthodox private life as well. She divorced her first husband and ran off to New Guinea with a New Zealander who rejoiced in the name of Reo Fortune, there to study childhood development and adolescence in the local tribes. In 1933 Mead studied three tribes, each of which had widely differing gender roles, which led her to believe that such roles are learned. She published these findings in her book *Sex and Temperament in Three Primitive Societies* (Mead, 1935). She divorced Fortune in 1935, then married one Gregory Bateson and set off again on her travels, this time to Indonesia. Despite having been told that she would never have children, she had one child with Bateson in 1939 and (characteristically) wrote a book about the experience.

Mead's work was certainly interesting and provided many insights into human behaviour, in particular the concept that culture is learned. Her work in New Guinea has been used as a major plank in the feminist cause, since it shows clearly that male domination is not the only natural order of things, but is simply one way of managing human affairs. On the other hand, some doubts were cast on Mead's work by later anthropologists, some of whom interviewed Mead's original respondents and were told that the tribes had systematically lied to her about their true behaviour. As Mead died in 1978, the truth is unlikely to be uncovered definitively, but since there is plenty of supporting evidence for Mead's initial research, the whole question is, as they say, academic.

Anthropology is not, of course, confined to Stone Age-type tribes living in tropical backwaters. Modern anthropologists are often recruited to explain human behaviour in business contexts, for example to explain how people communicate in the workplace. Any substantial group of people develop shared beliefs and behaviours. The problem for modern anthropologists is that industrial society is almost a single culture, distinguished only by languages and some minor variations in religion. The differences between the various citizens of the world are relatively small in comparison with the differences Mead observed between different tribes living in the same general area.

Geert Hofstede of Maastricht University carried out a very large international study in 1967 and 1973 in which he categorized different cultures across four dimensions: power distance, individualism, masculinity, and uncertainty avoidance. Power distance is the degree to which power and wealth is concentrated in the hands of a few people. Individualism refers to the degree to which people are able to break free of the normative pressures of the society around them, and the degree to which such behaviour is admired or reviled. Masculinity is the degree to which the society reinforces a traditional work model of male achievement, control and power, in other words the degree of differentiation of gender roles. Uncertainty avoidance is the degree to which the society has a lot of rules and regulations, removing the possibilities for plurality and chaos.

Hofstede later added another dimension, that of long-term orientation. This is the degree to which the society considers what might happen ten, twenty or fifty years from now. This dimension was added following a further study in which Chinese researchers added the Confucian dynamism concept, which is an interesting example of cultural dimensions being added to the research philosophy itself. Hofstede was able to categorize national cultures across his five dimensions, giving people a reasonable clue as to how someone from a given culture might respond to a particular set of circumstances (Hofstede, 1984).

Unfortunately, Hofstede's work has some major holes in it. First, the initial research was carried out some years ago – in the 1960s – and it does not take a genius to figure out that things have moved on quite a bit in the last forty years. In 1967 foreign travel was rare, and largely the province of the rich and the Navy. Nobody else went further than 50 miles for their holidays. In 1967 there were relatively few immigrants living in the UK. I remember how fascinated I was when an Indian restaurant opened up near my school – it was only about the third or fourth in London at the time. In 1967 the feminist movement was but a gleam in the eye of Germaine Greer. We hadn't even invented flower power, for criminy's sake. It would be naïve to suppose that cultural differences have not occurred in Britain since 1967, and equally naïve to suppose that other countries have not moved on a bit as well.

Secondly, Hofstede's research was carried out among employees of IBM. As the archetypal business monolith, IBM has a strong corporate culture – a stifling corporate culture, some say. The company has a policy of recruiting people who are typical IBM-ers, and then training them to be even more dedicated to the cause of shifting business equipment. The corporate culture would surely have had some effect on the respondents in Hofstede's research, but this has not apparently been considered by most of the people who quote his work.

Thirdly, one has to bear in mind that the differences between individuals from the same culture far outweigh the differences between the cultures themselves. The most individualistic Taiwanese is going to be much more individualistic than the least individualistic American, and in fact the overlap is considerable between the two populations. Therefore anyone who uses Hofstede's work as a sort of Rough Guide To Funny Foreigners is apt to be disappointed when confronted with an actual individual.

For marketers, anthropology would appear to be most relevant in circumstances where the main concern is mass communication or mass production. This is because culture deals with large groups of people (unlike sociology, which looks at smaller groups). A closer examination shows that in fact anthropology offers us insights into dealing with individuals from specific cultures, since the individual is influenced by the cultural environment. Some even argue that anthropology is about understanding the meaning systems that customers co-create with marketers, and certainly culture is heavily involved with creating meaning. Language is obviously about meaning, but even apart from language, almost everything about meaning is culturally-based.

Marketers deal with people in the mass as well as with individuals, and in many cases we use cultural references in our communications which would be incomprehensible to people from other cultures. This is particularly true, of course, in advertising, which is by its nature a mass communications device. In many cases, culture is shaped by the products themselves – anthropologists are clear about the ways in which available technology (i.e., tools and artefacts) shape the behaviour of a culture as much as the culture shapes the tools and artefacts. For example, the mobile telephone has reshaped the way individuals communicate, but the SMS system (texting) has created divergence within industrial cultures. An American friend recently asked me why Brits use text so much. I replied that it is a cheap way of sending a friend a message, and is convenient because the friend can read the message any time. My American chum was somewhat surprised at this, because text messaging is more expensive than voice telephoning in California, so hardly anybody uses it.

This divergence means that we will see, and probably already are seeing, differences in the way products are marketed in Britain as opposed to California. Some firms already make wide use of SMS for promotional purposes in the UK, whereas this is likely to be much less common in the USA. Even small firms use SMS. Swansea Sport Flying, a one-man flying school based at Swansea Airport, uses SMS to alert students when the weather is going to be good for flying, for example.

Much has been written, of course, about the communications revolution. Cheap electronics has been the defining characteristic of the early twenty-first century, and if the nineteenth century was a century of empire, the twentieth century the century of technological advance, then the twenty-first century bids fair to be the century of communication.

Technological advances have always shaped culture to some extent. The manufacture of cheap cars changed American culture in the early twentieth century: it was said at one time that half the children in America in the 1920s were conceived in the backs of Model T Fords, because for the first time courting couples were able to put distance between themselves and the watchful eyes of their parents. In an earlier age, the invention of photography led to the introduction of a new art form, and in prehistoric times the invention of tattooing enabled people to decorate their skins, thus identifying their tribal origin or even their profession.

In recent years people sometimes define themselves by the brands they buy. An interesting paper by Muniz and O'Guinn (2001) outlines how people develop new communities based around brands. We are all fairly familiar with the idea that modern society is breaking down traditional communities as people move around to find work, or marry outside their immediate geographical area. In fact, this idea has been around for a long time, and many nineteenth-century intellectuals thought that the whole concept of community was being destroyed by the inexorable advance of modernity.

Of course, it's always been the cry of the older generation that we are all going to Hell in a handbasket, and that 'things aren't what they used to be when I was young', which translates as 'things were better when I was young'. As it turns out, society has not come crashing down about our ears, we have simply re-condensed ourselves into different communities based on different cores. Some of these involve loyalty to a sports team (many women wonder why a man who can commit to Manchester United at the age of seven and remain loyal to them for his entire life even though he has not, technically, ever met them, has trouble making a commitment to marry the woman he plainly loves). Some involve shared interests, such as sports, arts or charity work. Muniz and O'Guinn (2001) consider what happens when communities coalesce around brands.

The authors use the Harley-Davidson motorcycle as an example. Harley riders do not buy the bike to get to work through the traffic: they buy the bike as a statement of who they are. This means that they need to behave in specific ways, buy specific clothes, become members of HOG (the Harley Owners' Group) and generally be Harley owners. If a Harley owner sees another Harley on the road, he (it is predominantly he) will wave a greeting, offer assistance at breakdowns, and so forth.

The authors also studied Apple Mac users and Saab drivers, and found a sense of community even when the individuals concerned lived far apart and had never met. What I particularly like about this study is that it shows the basic resilience of human beings. No matter what happens to change the world environment, we still like to get together and share our interests, help each other, and cut through barriers of wealth and class to do so.

> What is great about this country is that America started the tradition where the richest consumers buy essentially the same things as the poorest. You can be watching TV and see Coca-Cola, and you know that the President drinks Coke, Liz Taylor drinks Coke and, just think, you can drink Coke too. A Coke is a Coke and no amount of money can get you a better Coke than the one the bum on the corner is drinking. All Cokes are the same and all the Cokes are good. Liz Taylor knows it, the President knows it, the bum knows it, and you know it. (Warhol, 1975: 101)

Heartwarming, is it not?

other contributions from real sciences

Some subdivisions of existing behavioural sciences have contributed to marketing. For example, studies of communication have given us semiotics (the study of signs and the social construction of meaning), syntactics (the study of the structure of communication) and semantics (the study of the way words relate to external reality). Interestingly, marketing academics seldom seem to look in communications journals, at least judging from what one reads in textbooks and sees in lectures. For example, marketers still teach the Schramm model of communications (see Chapter 4) although it has been somewhat tarnished, if not actually discredited, in the fifty-odd years since it was first propounded.

Semiotics is more of a theoretical approach than an academic discipline. It is not limited to language, but most academics in the field use the spoken language as the main area of study, probably because speech is the most ambiguous and yet the most commonly used sign system for communication. The basic premise of semiotics is that meaning can only be derived socially: since meaning resides in people's minds, and is transferred from one mind to another (more or less) by the use of signs, social construction seems fairly obvious. Since misunderstanding abounds, however, we have to assume that the process is far from perfect. If telepathy exists (see Duke University above), students of semiotics might have to look for new work. For marketers, the importance of semiotics is that we have to use words and other signs which are accessible to our audience. In some cases this is not easy: some of our audience have specific jargon or slang which is accessible to them but not to others, and of course words change their meanings over time, or can change their meanings according to context. 'Wicked' is a prime example of this.

Syntactics considers the structure of communication. This is a constant source of anguish for textbook writers (trust me, I know) because no matter what order we put the chapters in, somebody thinks we have got it wrong. Structuring communications so that there is a story which the audience can follow makes communication of meaning much simpler. Symbols and signs change their meanings according to their position in the communication: a road safety poster showing a 10 year-old girl holding her father's hand to cross the road has a different meaning from a poster showing the same 10 year-old holding her 4 year-old brother's hand to cross the road. The second poster carries a much greater sense of vulnerability, even though the actual symbol (the little girl) is the same.

Structuring a communication comes to the fore in the case of teaser campaigns (those adverts where they show a meaningless message for a week or two, then follow it up with an explanation later). My favourite example of this is a teaser campaign my publisher did for one of my books. Over a period of about a month, they mailed out various items to marketing academics throughout the UK and parts of the continent. The first package contained a set of chopsticks with the message 'First you eat'. The second package, about a week later, contained a teabag with the message 'Then you drink'. The third package contained a fortune cookie, with the message 'Then you see your future'. The final package contained a sample chapter of the book, with a fortune cookie on the cover. The best thing about this campaign was that I had a lot of nice comments from colleagues in other universities. I had to point out that I had only written the book, the publishers had organized the campaign.

Recently, my wife bought me a book. This is not a common occurrence, because I have a lot of books and she doesn't always know what I already have in stock, but this book was special. It is a book of foreign brands, each of which has a humorous (or even obscene) meaning in English. Examples: Skum Confectionery from Sweden, Atum Bom tuna from Portugal, Slag beer from Holland. You'll have to buy the book to read the rude ones, of course. The fun of such names arises because the words do not relate to the external reality they are supposed to relate to: this is the province of semantics. Sometimes this means that the sources of words need to be traced. How did modern English evolve from the various languages which have contributed to it, for example? Sometimes semantics means looking at how words change their meanings over time, so that their relationship to reality also changes. The advice to international marketers is always to find a native speaker of the language of the country you are aiming for, and get them to vet everything before it goes out!

One of the most entertaining aspects of the study of signs is that the bulk of communication occurs in forms other than words. Silent communication is a study which spills over into cultural anthropology, since it involves a set of common understandings about what the gestures mean. For the foreign traveller, not understanding the gestures can cause great complications because the gestures are not always without meaning in the home context. For example, the Greek gesture for 'no' is a toss of the head accompanied by a clicking of the tongue. In the UK context, this would be a gesture of annoyance or frustration. The first time I saw this gesture, in Greece, was when a taxi driver wanted to indicate to me that he had no intention of going all the way out to Piraeus at this time of night. His simple 'no' came across to me as a gesture of irritation at the stupid foreigner, and I confess to feeling a little hurt by this. I recovered later when I saw the same gesture being used between Greeks, and I figured it out from the context. The problem with silent languages is that we assume that gestures and signs are universal – we assume that any deviations are due to stupidity or rudeness on the part of the foreigner. We don't tend to make that assumption about spoken language.

Communication theorists such as Rosengren (1999) view communication as an 'intersubjective, purposive interaction by means of doubly articulated human language based on symbols'. In other words, communication is purposeful, it is two-way, and it is based on symbols which signify elements of the total meaning. This definition differs from the orthodox definition of marketing communication, which usually centres around the idea that some kind of exchange is taking place. Most marketing communication is one-way, and a certain level of mental gymnastics is necessary to show how the interaction takes place. One has to assume that the recipient of the advertisement carries out a certain amount of mental processing in order to arrive at a meaning, but whether the meaning is the one the marketer intended is a horse of a different colour.

Canadian communications guru Marshall McLuhan is famous for telling us that 'the medium is the message' (McLuhan, 1964). McLuhan originally started out as a professor of English (despite having written in his diary, during his undergraduate years, that he would never become an academic). He fairly quickly moved towards studying the role of media, and by the 1960s was a well-known and charismatic figure. Unusually for an academic, he made a hit with the artists and musicians of the day, with the likes of Andy Warhol and John Lennon coming to visit him at the University of Toronto. McLuhan defined media as technological extensions of the body, which places all communication firmly on a human level. Seen from this perspective, marketing communications move from a discussion of whether to use TV or press or billboards, back to a conversation between someone who is 'in the business' and someone who is not.

One can't help feeling that McLuhan would have liked the current near-universal ownership of mobile phones. As a medium, mobiles are clearly technological extensions of the body – they are personal, they are portable, and they are ubiquitous. I always liked McLuhan because of his neat way of coming out with aphorisms. He was the darling of the hippy era when he came out with statements such as:

'Mud sometimes gives the illusion of depth.'

'We look at the present through a rear-view mirror. We march backwards into the future.'

'Only puny secrets need protection. Big discoveries are protected by public incredulity.'

McLuhan died of a stroke in 1980, aged only 69.

A surprise entry in the science of marketing is statistics. I say it's a surprise entry because most students who sign up for marketing courses do so with confidence that they will not have to do hard sums. After all, marketing's just about designing nice ads, isn't it? Unfortunately for them, marketing research comes loping round the corner, eyes flashing and teeth gnashing, to bite them on the posterior.

Marketing research and academic research both use statistical tools to analyse data, and learning how to manipulate data statistically is sometimes taught on marketing courses. Statistics came as a nasty surprise to me, too, but I overcame my initial horror and found that actually statistics can be fun (er … maybe not fun, exactly, but manageable). In the main, practical marketers use only a few of the main statistical tools: the Student's t-test, occasionally a chi-square test, and some sampling methods. The purpose of these statistical tools is to try to ensure that the results obtained from a research exercise can be relied upon reasonably well. Academics use a great many more statistical devices, often in an attempt to extract meaningful results from small samples or otherwise flawed data. Sometimes this works, sometimes not.

One of the most common statistical tools is the Student's t-test. This tells us the extent to which the results can be relied on to have come about by something other than chance, and it gives us a confidence level (often expressed as a percentage). The t-test compares the variation between the samples with the sample size and returns a statement to the effect that we can be (say) 97 per cent sure that the variation is real, not just a fluke result. Normally anything less than 95 per cent would mean that we should really collect more data – the bigger the sample size, the more reliable the results.

The t-test was invented by one William Sealy Gosset, who was employed by the Guinness brewery in Dublin. His job involved sampling the beer (for analysis purposes) and drawing conclusions about the whole batch from a small sample. Unfortunately for Gosset, Guinness did not allow its employees to publish their work, because the company did not want its competitors to have access to what they regarded as trade secrets. Gosset therefore published his work under the pen-name, The Student. Hence Student's t-test, rather than Gosset's t-test. Gosset died in 1937, without having the t-test rightfully attributed to him under his own name.

Sadly, the teaching of statistics (or anything mathematical) is rapidly disappearing from business studies courses, because most students have not been taught basic mathematics in school (or anywhere else) and many of them have difficulty even with simple arithmetic. This stores up problems for the future, of course. Many students find themselves in trouble when they try to carry out research for their dissertations. On the plus side, the nice people at Microsoft have developed easy-to-use statistical packages which do all the hard work. So, provided students understand the theory behind the tools and understand what the results mean, they can generate useful research outcomes.

Marketing's relationship with real sciences has been basically the same as that between ram raiders and retailers. Marketing academics have run in, grabbed some useful ideas, and run out again never to return. Once we had our own journals about consumer behaviour, market research, marketing communications, and so forth, we almost never returned to the real-science journals on psychology, sociology, statistics, communications, anthropology, or whatever. We had become a real science, or so we thought. The next section of the book will therefore look at marketing as a proper subject of its own.

Part II

Marketing as a Proper Subject

3

The Marketing Gurus and Some of Their Thinking

Throughout the history of commerce, there have been people who have tried to analyse what is happening, in the hope of improving practice in the industries they observe. Of course, they also hope to spend their lives sitting around thinking beautiful thoughts rather than actually going out and getting some real work done. Marketing is no exception. It has its fair share of pundits, gurus, theorists and intellectuals, most of whom contradict each other and even themselves on occasion.

The history of marketing thought (or perhaps the history of thinking about marketing) goes back a long way. In Chapter 1 we saw how the economists began the whole process, and in Chapter 2 we saw how marketers are able to lift ideas from behavioural scientists in order to modify their thinking appropriately. There are two threads to mainstream marketing guruism: there is the history of marketing itself (that is, what we imagine is the history of marketing practice) and there is the history of academic marketing theory (which does not necessarily correspond with what is happening in the real world).

Keith (1960) provided us with an interesting model of how marketing practice developed. This analysis was based on the Pillsbury Dough Company, a large American flour milling company. Keith said that the company had gone through three distinct paradigms in the course of developing a marketing concept. These were as follows:

1. *The production era.* At this time the capacity of the mills rather than customer need was what drove the market. The reason for this was that the market was growing rapidly, so that demand outstripped supply.

2. *The sales era*. During this period, the company regarded an effective, fast-talking salesforce as the way to control the market.
3. *The marketing era*. At this time the company was driven by customer need.

Although this model was referring to a very specific company at a very specific time, it has been seized upon by marketing academics and, with some adaptations, is still the main model quoted in all the textbooks and on all the courses. The reason for this is that it is simple to teach – to be fair to Keith, he did not intend it to be regarded as a history of marketing, but it's such a neat model it would be a shame to let reality get in the way of it.

The critiques of this view have been many. In 1988 Fullerton put forward two main arguments against the idea that the nineteenth century was characterized by the production era. First, said Fullerton, it ignores the historical facts about business conditions at the time, which were in fact unstable and often characterized by sharp falls in demand. In fact, there were several major depressions between 1870 and 1920. Secondly, the production-era idea assumes that demand was stimulated by production, in other words that consumers would immediately rush out and buy products as soon as they saw them. In fact, the nineteenth century was characterized by some very aggressive marketing activities, notably some extremely pushy shop assistants and a great deal of advertising activity, much of which made outrageous claims about the products or even made scurrilous accusations about competitors' products.

The evidence against the existence of a sales era is also compelling. Marketing activities were well-established long before the sales era was supposed to have occurred, and in practice it was obvious that many companies were already considering customers' needs (or at least paying lip-service to them) during this era. This is not so very different from the situation which prevails in the twenty-first century. The hard-sell techniques which supposedly characterized the sales era (and which we are supposed to have left behind) are certainly still in use nowadays, and the problem-solving approach used nowadays worked even in the so-called sales era.

Of course, one could argue that the development of marketing refers to a general paradigm, that is to say that most companies during each of the periods concerned was operating under the production paradigm, or the sales paradigm, or whatever: the prevailing climate of business might be that one or other paradigm comes to the fore, even though there are exceptions. This type of argument is always good fun because it allows one to ignore any evidence that inconveniently gets in the way of the theory.

Gilbert and Bailey (1990) re-thought the history of marketing and proposed a somewhat more enlightened view of the process. Even this view of commercial history is likely to be flawed, of course. History is not a neat process, nor is it possible to be definitive about what happened hundreds of years ago (or even last week). However, Gilbert and Bailey appear to have at least an alternative view. This is as follows:

1. *The era of antecedents* (1500–1750). During this period commerce developed from an activity which was regarded as little better than larceny to a (moderately) respectable profession. This period also saw the growth of capitalism, whereby people with money could invest in profitable enterprises, or even in unprofitable ones, without actually having to manage the business. The separation of management from investment was an important step in professionalizing managers, of course.

2. *The era of origins* (1750–1850). During this period the basic concepts of marketing began to develop. Segmentation and advertising began to grow in importance, competition became intense, and markets became considerably less stable.

3. *The era of institutional development* (1850–1930). During this period specialist institutions such as large retailers and wholesalers, commercial services such as accountants and lawyers, and specialist distribution systems such as rail and road freight transporters grew up to serve the burgeoning needs of industry.

4. *The era of refinement and formalization* (1930–present). During this period the academics got involved, and marketing became a proper science, with its own journals and research programmes. Consequently, marketing also became a distinct profession, with trained marketers who had degrees and diplomas in the subject.

Since the early 1960s marketing has been largely concerned with consumer behaviour. If we can figure out what makes people buy things, we can figure out better ways of making sure they buy our things rather than our competitors' things, to the greater good of all. During this period, the balance of power has moved away from manufacturers and towards retailers, probably because retailers are closer to the customers and can respond more quickly to customer needs. At the same time, retailers have become very much larger, and manufacturing has withered on the vine as we have moved towards a post-industrial society (at least in Western Europe, the USA, and the other so-called industrialized nations). This shift of the balance of power further down the distribution chain has had some fairly marked effects on the way marketers do business.

marketing theory

Initially, marketing was regarded as a function of the business – a professional service which concentrated on advertising, personal selling, public relations, and sales promotion. Bringing consistency and cohesiveness to marketing, and integrating the contributions made by other disciplines, was the main aim of marketing gurus. The intention was to ensure that marketers in the real world could have a set of tools and models which would work every time. During this period the core concepts of marketing were identified, codified, packaged and sold to the eagerly waiting world. This period was called a period of reconception by Bartels (1976). He says that this period produced the following ideas:

1. The input–output view of marketing systems.
2. The understanding that economics does not have all the answers.
3. The notion of competitive advantage as a result of marketing.
4. The view of marketing as being concerned with managing exchange.

Because academics seemed so sure that they knew what they were doing, and because much of the research published at the time was expressed in numbers, people began to believe that marketers were magicians who could push people's buttons and thus rule the world. This functional managerialism was fostered by some marketers, who put forward the view that markets can be manipulated (or even controlled) for the benefit of the marketers and their companies.

Key thinkers during the reconceptualization process set out to answer the most important marketing questions of the time:

1. What is marketing about?
2. What does marketing involve?
3. What is marketing trying to do?

I will now try to outline the ways each of the main thinkers have contributed to answering those questions. These marketing gurus are to be envied: they have managed, in the main, to create a very nice life for themselves in the 'beautiful thoughts' business, an achievement which most academics would hope to emulate.

McCarthy

E. Jerome McCarthy is usually credited with inventing the four P model of the marketing mix (product, price, place, promotion) (McCarthy, 1960). This is probably an example of crediting an individual with a discovery which was actually made by several other people beforehand – and even subsequently. Borden (1964) conceptualized marketing as a process of planning, implementation and control but included a total of 12 elements in his marketing mix. This was obviously far too complex for the emerging 'airport bookshop' school of management, so the hunt was on for a shorter, snappier set of mix elements. Various alternatives were considered and rejected (Frey, 1961; Howard, 1957; Lazer & Kelly, 1962), but finally McCarthy's 1960 set of four Ps was adopted and remains to this day the accepted wisdom. For a while in the 1990s there was a fashion for adding more Ps as the shortcomings of the model became clearer. A lot of marketing journals in the 1990s have papers entitled 'Pork chops – the fifth P of marketing?', or something similar, but the vast majority of research output and the vast majority of marketing textbooks follow the four P approach.

The model is useful for teaching because it pigeonholes marketing tactics into neat one-hour-lecture chunks, but it leaves out many other marketing-type activities, such as market research, strategic planning, customer relations, and so forth. Borden thought that his 12 elements were far from comprehensive, so it is fairly obvious that reducing the list to only four elements is a gross over-simplification.

The marketing mix approach (whether it is a four P model, a seven P model, a 12-element model or whatever) has a certain appeal in terms of simplifying the problem, because the actual subject of marketing encompasses so many different elements that it is almost impossible to find a way through the jungle. On the other hand, the mix has been widely criticized on the basis that it conflicts fundamentally with the marketing concept: it implies that marketing is something that is done to people, rather than something that is done for people.

McCarthy is still with us, and he is still teaching and writing: his introductory marketing book (2004, co-authored with William Perreault) is still in print.

Theodore Levitt

Levitt has been a remarkable thinker about marketing. He has entertained us for forty-odd years with his wacky notions, most of which have turned out to be right on the money and have become mainstream thinking within a very short time. In 1960 he wrote a seminal article called 'Marketing Myopia', published in the *Harvard Business Review*, in which he laid out the bare bones of the marketing concept. In the article he said that 'selling focuses on the needs of the seller, marketing on the needs of the buyer'. This view has been widely misrepresented, incidentally. Marketing is not concerned with seeing off the salesforce, it is concerned with refocusing everybody on customer needs (Levitt, 1960).

'Marketing Myopia' was an attempt to move marketing away from being a function within the firm (a way of persuading people to buy stuff) and move it towards being the driving philosophy of the firm (an orientation towards customers). The marketing concept (as conceived by Levitt) comprises customer orientation, integration of effort on a company-wide basis, and profitability rather than sales volume as a measure of corporate success. The article was one of the most influential ever written, and it changed the way marketers thought about the entire process.

Levitt later contributed to the conceptualization of relationship marketing (Levitt, 1983). He pointed out that marketing thought focuses mainly on the single transaction rather than on the lifetime value of the customer. Cozying up to the existing customers is greatly to be preferred over the more difficult and more expensive activity of wooing new customers. This idea has great appeal, and there is research to back up the theory (although it is hard to track down). The idea that it is five times as expensive to recruit a new customer as it is to retain an old one is widely quoted, and it sounds sensible enough. After all, the existing customers already know all about us, and (we hope) are happy with what we do. This should, if there is any justice in the world, encourage them to stay with us.

Levitt was especially keen to consider the relationship as being akin to courtship and marriage. He said that firms and their customers meet up somewhere, go through a period of getting to know each other better (at the beginning of which a certain amount of poetic licence is expected when discussing what one has done or is about to do), and finally the happy couple form a successful long-term relationship. This view of relationship marketing is still widely taught and is regarded as a good analogy, although it doesn't really stand up to close scrutiny. After all, most firms seek to establish relationships with a lot of different customers. Don't try this in a marriage.

In a period of shrinking markets, increasing competition, and increased reluctance on the part of buyers, relationship marketing has found a ready audience. The idea that we can avoid all the uncertainty and hassle of trying to persuade someone to join us, and instead simply hang on to the existing customer base, is understandably attractive: what we have to do to keep the customers, and how we decide which are worth keeping and which should be thrown a concrete lifebelt, are but two of the practical difficulties involved.

Levitt's contribution to marketing thought is sporadic, but always worth waiting for. He is a clear thinker, with thought-provoking ideas which other people can then run with. As a starter of rabbits for other dogs to chase, he is second to none.

Peter Drucker

Drucker was essentially a management guru, but he gradually became a marketing guru once he saw which way the wind was blowing. He is famously quoted as saying 'We are all marketers now', and for stating that the sole function of any business is to create a customer. He also said that 'There will, one assumes, always be a need for some selling, but the purpose of marketing is to make selling unnecessary' (Drucker, 1973). Like Levitt's quote, this has also been misinterpreted as meaning that the salesforce must go, and that right quickly. Naturally, salespeople resent any such moves, and since most salespeople think that they should be running the show anyway, one can readily see where conflict might arise.

Drucker contributed a great deal towards bringing marketing into the boardroom. His view that customers are what businesses make helped shift the focus away from engineering. Boards began to consider the much wider possibilities, especially in the competitive arena. As a strategist, Drucker saw the importance of positioning the company to make best use of its assets in terms of creating customers. Here is another Drucker quote: 'Marketing is so basic that it cannot be considered a separate function. It is the whole business, seen from the viewpoint of its final result, that is, from the customer's point of view' (1973).

This way of looking at the business moved marketing up the agenda at the same time as it moved marketers down the agenda. If everybody is a marketer, and everybody is looking towards customer centrality, where does that leave the professional marketers? This remains as a knotty problem for practitioners, especially in a world where everyone thinks they know how to flog stuff.

His ability to convey his views in a cogent and accessible manner made him the darling of the lecture circuit. His approach was simple and easily absorbed by his audiences, and his thinking was well ahead of its time. He died, aged 96, in 2005.

Stephen Brown

Two or three years ago I was taken by surprise at a conference. I had expected my co-author to be presenting our paper, but he turned out not to be on the list of delegates. In fact, not only was he not on the list, he wasn't coming. So there I was, with nothing prepared, and an audience of leading marketing academics from the UK, the rest of Europe, Australia, New Zealand, and even a few stray Americans. What was I to do?

Well, I've been in this business a few years, and I have occasionally been known to have left my lecture notes on the train, so I did what any old warhorse would do: I busked it. I read through the paper, made a few notes, and armed only with some dry-wipe markers and a chunk of cheek I presented the paper. Often at conferences my papers are not well-attended. Not everyone is interested in my research area, which is exhibitions and trade fairs, but on this occasion the room I was in was packed to the ceiling and people were leaning in through the doorway. My natural feelings of gratification at this apparently flattering turnout were quickly dampened, however, when I saw that Stephen Brown was going to perform immediately after me.

Stephen is the performing flea of British marketing. His presentations are always packed, and his writings are seized upon by an eager audience. He is always lively, thought-provoking and irreverent. Watching Stephen present is rather like throwing a lighted match into a box of fireworks – you quickly become aware that something exciting but rather disturbing is about to happen.

Hidden behind the smoke and mirrors, though, is some serious academic thought. Stephen has been credited with inventing the Wheel of Retailing, which may or may not be to his credit since it does not stand up well to close examination. More recently he has become known for applying postmodern philosophy to marketing.

If you are entirely *au fait* with postmodernism, you have an intellectual treat in store. If you have never heard of it, some explanation will be necessary. Postmodernism follows on (surprise surprise) from modernism. Modernism is the view that the human race is progressing, growing, moving towards a wonderful future from a somewhat unpleasant past. This has been the prevailing view in marketing: one needs only to look at the Boston Consulting Group Matrix to see that marketers do not anticipate ever seeing a shrinking market. Modernism is typified by the word 'progress', according to Stephen Brown, and indeed it is a philosophy which embraces individualism, freedom, advancement, and a rejection of the hidebound past represented by religion, myth and tradition. Sounds good so far, huh?

Unfortunately, the human race is fairly obviously not on a roll. We still get involved in pointless wars, we still have recessions, we still make mistakes and we still end up backtracking a lot. What's more, we still find ourselves yearning for a glorious past which probably never existed anyway. This is where postmodernism comes in, and also where Stephen comes in.

Postmodernists say that we are *not* on a continual climb to the sunlit uplands. In fact, we are not progressing at all, merely living in the present and doing our best. Different ways of life, different styles, different attitudes are all mixed in together in a pluralist world: there is no dominant style. At the same time, the future and the past become confused, and we may well move towards the past (Stephen talks about retro design such as the new Volkswagen Beetle as an example of how postmodernism affects marketing) or try to live in the future (becoming a Trekky, for example). There is a cultural propensity to juxtapose almost anything with almost anything else, whether it fits or not. (Salsa music, for example, is a fusion of jazz and Latin music, and I recall a memorable dinner in Hawaii which was a Japanese–Californian fusion of seared tuna and avocado. Weird, but it worked. The restaurant décor was also an eclectic mix of Japanese, Californian, and pre-war influences.) Postmodernists also believe that chaos and disequilibria are normal (rather than order and equilibrium), which again is pretty much what happens in conditions of hypercompetition (see Richard D'Aveni, below).

Almost all postmodern ideas seem to fit extremely well with the current state of play in marketing. Stephen Brown points out that consumption and production are reversed – people define themselves by what they consume, not by what they produce – and the emphasis in the developed world (the post-industrial world) is mainly on consumption. Few of us produce anything in any physical sense. Then again, there is a lack of commitment (very postmodern) in which people are reluctant to commit to anything at all, whether it's an idea or a brand or a project.

The features of postmodernism, and their relationship to marketing, are as follows. This list is based on Firat and Shultz (1997), and was passed on to me by my friend and colleague Maurice Patterson.

1. *Openness/tolerance*. This is the acceptance of different styles and ways of living without prejudice or evaluations of superiority or inferiority. In marketing, this openness to new ideas

has made it much easier to find 'new, improved' products simply by transferring ideas in from other cultures. This is especially true in the food industry.

2. *Hyperreality*. This is the constitution of social reality through hype. Hyperreality refers to overstatement: for example, the slogan 'Rowntrees Fruit Pastilles Take You Beyond Fruit' is hyperreal. Marketers do this all the time, so much so that UK law refers to 'advertising puff' as being acceptable in law (as opposed to flat-out lies, which aren't).

3. *Perpetual present*. In the postmodern world, we experience everything in the present, whether it is the past or the future we are considering. We have no problem in thinking about the 1960s (the TV show *Heartbeat* being an example) without requiring a great deal of historical accuracy. We also have no problem experiencing the future (*Startrek*, *Stargate*, *Star Wars*, anything else with Star in the title) as if it were the present.

4. *Paradoxical juxtapositions*. This is the California–Japanese restaurant thing. It is also the odd phraseology that wine experts might be expected to use. For example 'This is a cheeky little wine, with hints of camomile and overtones of tar. Definitely an Alec Guinness rather than an Arnold Schwarzenegger.' For marketers, the possibilities are endless, and telling the difference between Boot's the Chemist and WH Smith the newsagents is actually quite difficult. They sell mainly the same stuff, in a stream of paradoxical juxtapositions (a great phrase to use at parties).

5. *Fragmentation*. The omnipresence of disjointed and disconnected moments and experiences in life. Markets have become more dynamic, and therefore more fragmented: people are not happy with the same product everybody else owns, they want something new and different.

6. *Lack of commitment*. There is a cultural unwillingness to commit to any single idea or project. This is clearly problematical for marketers, since we seek to generate loyalty and involvement with our customers. Since marketers are actually human, it is possible that they are themselves unprepared to

commit to customers, so we are perhaps losing ground a bit on that account.

7. *Decentring of the subject.* Removal of the human being from the central importance he or she had in modern culture, and the increasing acceptance of the potentials of his or her objectification. Individuals are not in control. In marketing situations, the consumers have to do as they are told if they want to enjoy the benefits of consumption. Failure to follow the instructions may result in injury or death, but we aren't telling you which bits of the instructions are life-and-death and which are merely inserted because we thought it might make life easier for you or would protect the equipment. We especially aren't telling you which instructions are only there to protect us from American product liability laws and are therefore intended for the courtroom (for example, do not touch the circular saw blade while it is rotating).

8. *Reversal of consumption and production.* This is the idea that value is created by consumption, not production. There is some sense in this from a marketer's viewpoint: if a product is a bundle of benefits, it only becomes valuable at the time when the benefits happen, that is when the product is used. Electric drills have no real value if they are simply left in a warehouse until they rot. They do have value when they are poking holes in things.

9. *Emphasis on form and style.* Form and style are more important than content in determining meaning and life. The entire fashion industry is based on this concept, as is much of the food industry. The King Prawn Ring is a fine example of a product (frozen king prawns with frozen sauce) where the presentation is more important than the content. The neat circle of prawns, with the sauce in the middle ready for dipping, actually works out at £7.65 a kilo, whereas the king prawns themselves are considerably cheaper when bought separately.

10. *Acceptance of disorder and chaos.* The idea that chaos is normal, and that we actually cannot create order out of

chaos, is one which is catching on fast. For marketing strategists the idea might be disturbing since there is a great deal of planning which will have to be scrapped, but for some marketers (notably Richard D'Aveni) the notion of chaos as the norm is a vindication.

Stephen Brown did not invent postmodernism, nor is he the only marketer to have taken on its basic philosophy and considered the implications. He is the guy who wrote the book, though, and even wrote a sequel which has also sold extremely well.

Last time I saw Stephen he was presenting his latest paper. Dressed as a wizard, he was expounding the merits of Marketing for Muggles, based on the Harry Potter books and films, and seemed to be having a great time. A paradoxical juxtaposition if ever I saw one.

Richard D'Aveni

Richard D'Aveni is not actually a marketer (he is a lawyer and accountant), but he is known as the guru in charge of hypercompetition (a concept originally credited to Michael Porter). Hypercompetition is a state of affairs in which there is an oversupply of the product, and competition goes beyond the somewhat gentlemanly process described in most strategy books and goes into a condition where the key to success lies in developing a long series of short-term advantages.

To expand, the traditional view of competition is that there are market leaders, market followers, market nichers and market challengers. Apart from the challengers, everybody else is fairly satisfied with the status quo and stays pretty much where they are – it is not in anyone's interests to rock the boat. In a hypercompetitive environment, though, everyone is jockeying for position, and the aim is to destabilize the market in the hopes of gaining a temporary advantage. The gloves are off, in other words.

D'Aveni says that there are four dimensions of competition: price and quality, timing and know-how, stronghold creation and invasion, and deep pockets. He then goes on to talk about the 'new 7-Ss', a reference to the 7-S framework beloved by Peters and Waterman. D'Aveni, like Peters and Waterman, has struggled a bit to find seven words beginning with S which describe his model, but airport bookstalls require us to find neat little *aides-mémoire* for the jetlagged businessmen and wannabes who buy our books, so here goes:

1. *Superior stakeholder satisfaction.* Providing stakeholders with a better deal than that obtaining from competitors is always a winner, but at what cost? Some firms have gained an instant advantage by dropping their prices dramatically (and temporarily), a situation which is sustainable if the firm has a 'deep pockets' advantage, but which cuts profits even more dramatically.
2. *Strategic soothsaying.* Soothsaying implies forecasting the future by unreliable or unscientific means. Strategic soothsaying is about seeking out new possible markets which the competition does not currently see.
3. *Speed.* Being able to move swiftly and adapt quickly to new competitive environments is a key issue in hypercompetition, because the environment is inherently unstable.
4. *Surprise.* Taking the competition by surprise is at the base of all hypercompetition.
5. *Shifting the rules of competition.* In most markets, rules have been agreed, if only by common consent. Hypercompetitors seek to break the rules at every opportunity, throwing 'gentlemen's agreements' out of the window.
6. *Signalling strategic intent.* This is about letting competitors know what you have planned, with the aim of either stalling their own initiatives or of creating uncertainty which in turn can erode competitors' ability to defend against attacks.
7. *Simultaneous and sequential thrusts.* Hitting competitors with a new initiative before they have had time to respond to the last one creates further confusion and erodes the competitors' positions. Intel have a policy of having the next-generation chip

ready before the first one is launched so that competitive responses can be pre-empted more easily.

In most markets, hypercompetition is not an issue, but it may become more important as time goes by. Customers are not as loyal as they once were, and there are more firms starting up every day, hence more competitors. The clarity of D'Aveni's thinking might have been clouded somewhat by the necessity to fit everything into seven Ss, but no doubt the sales of the book will have been helped – everybody wants to be a one-minute manager, which includes having easily remembered rules and models.

For academic marketers, hypercompetition is a threat on two fronts. First, the strategic planning model might as well be flushed down the toilet since there is no real way of predicting what will happen next. Secondly, marketing is likely to be relegated to a tactical role as the firm makes rapid responses and attacks rather than builds on its solid customer base. D'Aveni has been accused of being jingoistic, simplistic, Cassandra-like, blinkered, and a talker of rubbish, but if he's right about hypercompetition (and many marketers think he is), then we are going to have to be on our toes and ready for anything the competition might hurl at us. Personally, I suspect there is a degree of hype about hypercompetition (if you forgive the pun). I can certainly see evidence of it in the USA, but in cuddly old Britain? Not so far. As consumers become more demanding, though, I can see where it might arrive here.

Shelby Hunt

Shelby Hunt has been trying to develop a unified model of competition. He is a great man for criticizing the way academics operate in 'silos', ignoring each others' research and thinking. So much is published annually in academic journals that one cannot really blame academics for not reading everything that they might – like the Red Queen in *Alice Through the Looking Glass*, it takes all the running we can do to stay in the same place.

Having said that, Shelby Hunt has done a commendable job in blending economics, marketing, behavioural sciences, and you name it to come up with the conclusion that competition is about resources and natural competitive advantage. This may seem to be obvious, but in fact Shelby leads us through a convoluted route, looking at several other disciplines on the way, and the conclusions are none the worse for it.

Whether this is truly marketing, or whether it is edging over into business strategy, is really a question about the scope of marketing. This is covered more fully in Chapter 4, but it is a 'hot issue' for marketers and one which will not readily be answered. Shelby Hunt's own contribution to the debate, in a seminal paper published in 1976, is that all marketing questions can be categorized in terms of three dichotomies: profit vs. non-profit, macro vs. micro, and positive vs. normative. This gives a total of eight boxes into which marketing issues can be placed (Hunt, 1976). Hunt said in the paper that he recognized that there would still be a great deal of debate about what belongs in which box, and whether some things were really marketing or not, but the boxes did at least give some kind of structure to what was, at the time, a somewhat formless and even chaotic discipline.

Shelby Hunt also offered a major contribution to our thinking about marketing theory itself. In 1983 he carried out a review of definitions of theory, and defined marketing theory as follows:

> A theory is a systematically related set of statements, including some lawlike generalizations that are empirically testable. The purpose of theory is to increase scientific understanding through a systematized structure capable of both explaining and predicting phenomena. (Hunt, 1983)

Although this idea of theory is based on a positivist perspective (see Chapter 5), it has remained the basic research paradigm for academic marketers.

Finally, with his former PhD student Robert Morgan, Shelby Hunt published a paper on relationship marketing. This paper became the most widely-cited paper of the decade in which it was published (even though it was rejected outright by the first journal they sent it to). The paper was entitled, 'The Commitment–Trust Theory of Relationship Marketing' and, in true Hunt fashion, it involved a wide range of contributions from other disciplines. Drawing on sociological and anthropological studies of marriage, the authors decided that commitment and trust were the essential bases of all relationships, including business relationships (Morgan and Hunt, 1994). Not something that you couldn't have thought of for yourself, perhaps, but like his work on competition, Shelby has a nice way of stating the obvious in very conceptually precise terms. Like many other ideas, it's only obvious when someone tells you – and Shelby tells you in such a nice way.

Jagdish Sheth

Or Jag, as he is known to his fellow-marketers. Jag Sheth is probably best known for his complex model of consumer behaviour, co-authored with John Howard (Howard and Sheth, 1969). This model is still widely taught because it encompasses almost everything that consumers do and think when making purchase decisions, so it pops up in most marketing courses, especially consumer behaviour courses. Sheth says that he learned about consumer behaviour by helping out in his brother's shop when he was a teenager, but this is a story which seems a little too good to be true.

In more recent years, Sheth has turned his attention to competition theory and marketing strategy. He recently published a book called *The Rule of Three*, in which he propounds the theory that, in most markets, the three largest companies control between 70 per cent and 90 per cent of the market (Sheth and Sisodia, 2002). This is not exactly rocket science: it is similar to the Pareto Principle, otherwise known as the 80/20 rule, which purports to show that 20 per cent of anything controls, owns or accounts for 80 per cent of something else. In other words, it's a fine example of airport bookshop business books, except that it doesn't tell us much we didn't already have a pretty good idea about.

Among academics, Sheth is better known for his view that we should be publishing for the benefit of practitioners, not for other academics. He says he would rather be in the *Harvard Business Review* or the *Wall Street Journal* than in the *Journal of Marketing* or the *Journal of Consumer Behaviour*. This is a view with which I have a great deal of sympathy: I don't think we should regard our job as over when we have published in a top-flight academic journal. We should go on to publish in practitioner journals and the business press, otherwise what are we for? The taxpayer isn't paying us to talk to each other – and anyway, who reads academic journals? Teaching is only part of the story – by the time students have risen through the ranks of their companies enough to have any influence, they have forgotten whatever we told them. This is probably just as well, in view of the fact that we are probably years out of date anyway.

Sheth, like Kotler, believes that marketing should broaden its scope and should be looking towards marketing ideas, services, non-profit organizations, and even whole countries. He says that this should help reduce the negative view people have of marketing (though I don't see that this, in itself, should be a motivation for broadening what we do – this isn't a popularity contest). I suspect it might also help Jag Sheth sell more books, but hey, that's marketing!

Philip Kotler

Kotler is the Grand Old Man of marketing, a prolific writer and teacher, and an influence on generations of marketing students. His books are used worldwide, and he has even developed the idea of franchising his name – it appears on several books, as co-author, where his actual writing input has not been all that large. Now in his seventies, he is probably the most influential marketer of all time.

Kotler is an affable old cove, and has been the main advocate of expanding the boundaries of marketing for the last umpteen years. He invented societal marketing, which encourages marketers to think of society as a whole when marketing goods, and seems to have no trouble reconciling the inevitable conflicts this approach generates. He also advocates considering marketing as the management of exchange, rather than as a way of shifting product, and he has picked up the Drucker torch of customer centrality. He is largely responsible for the idea of considering marketing as a way of meeting customer needs, moving the focus away from price and distribution and on to the consumer. In 1969, he published a seminal paper with a chap called Levy, in which he advocated broadening the scope of marketing, taking it beyond merely shifting product for profit-making corporations and moving it on into the sunlit uplands of not-for-profit marketing, and anything else involving exchange (Kotler & Levy, 1969).

He was also credited with developing the concept of the marketing audit, which is a snapshot of the firm's current marketing activities and position. This is a key concept in developing marketing strategy, and is also a useful checklist for anyone working as a marketing consultant.

In his writing, Kotler has a penchant for ever longer and more comprehensive definitions of things. His latest definition of marketing has become almost incomprehensible in its completeness. It goes something like this:

> Marketing is a social and managerial process by which individuals and groups obtain what they need and want through creating and exchanging products and value with each other.

This definition (which will probably have changed and had more 'ands' inserted by the time you read this) covers pretty much all human interaction. Are we creating value and exchanging it with each other when we marry someone? Yes of course. Have children together? Yes, of course. Invite friends round for dinner? Certainly. Play a practical joke on a friend? Surely. Are these marketing? Hmmm ....

Kotler takes very much a managerial view of marketing, that it is about managing exchange, and he has been criticized for looking at marketing as something that is done *to* customers rather than something that is done *for* them. I think this criticism is somewhat unkind: after all, Kotler invented societal marketing, which is clearly a socially responsible view of how marketing should be conducted. Not to mention that somebody has to take charge of the process, even if we are doing something for people.

Malcolm MacDonald

Malcolm MacDonald is Emeritus Professor of Marketing at Cranfield, a post which is richly deserved. As one of the UK's leading marketers, Malcolm has been instrumental in moving marketing up the agenda for practitioners. He is a strategist, and is a hot-shot on marketing planning (about which he has written several entertaining books).

Professor MacDonald's main contribution has been in bridging the gap between academics and practitioners. He is respected as an academic, but he has still managed to produce 38 books, most of them 'how-to' guides to marketing. Retaining academic rigour while being engaging enough for practitioners is no small feat, but he has retained his connections with practice by the simple expedient of continuing to be a company director and consultant while working for Cranfield. He works with the boards of directors of companies such as Xerox, IBM and BP, and gives seminars and workshops to practitioners worldwide. I say simple – it must take considerable time management skills to make it all work.

As a contributor to theory, Malcolm MacDonald is notably low key. In fact it is hard to find anything that he has added. What he has done for marketing, and for industry, is to talk a lot of common sense about the subject and do so to people who are actually in a position to make it all work. Emeritus Professor means that he has retired, but they still want to keep him on the books – a wise move for an institution which prides itself on not living half-way up an ivory tower.

A few years back, I watched him have a debate with John Saunders at an Academy of Marketing conference. It was a performance worth watching: John Saunders is no slouch, but Malcolm wiped the floor with him in the debate (all very good-natured, I may say). I like people who recognize that marketing is about practice, not about developing ever more complex theories, and Malcolm MacDonald achieves that in spades.

Richard P. Bagozzi

A long time ago, twenty years at least, I was working up towards doing a PhD or at least an MPhil. My prospective supervisor advised me to take a look at some American PhDs because at that time there were few, if any, marketing PhDs in the UK. The only one I could find was Richard P. Bagozzi's. For the life of me, I can't remember what it was about, and it wasn't any help reading it anyway, but I have often tripped over Dr Bagozzi's papers since, and reflected that I knew him way back when.

In all probability you could go right through a marketing course, even to Masters level, and never hear of Richard P. Bagozzi. He is, however, something of an important figure to marketing academics because he has been at the sharp end of the debate about what marketing is and is not. He defines the core research question of marketing as 'what are the forces and conditions resolving marketing exchange relationships?', which should keep us going for a few years at least. If this is the question, the implication is that the distinctive core, or focus, of marketing is exchange. Bagozzi went on to say that marketing is the discipline of exchange behaviour, which puts him pretty much in the camp of 'marketing is everything'.

Bagozzi goes on to argue that there are three types of exchange – restricted, generalized and complex – and that exchange relationships carry three types of meaning – utilitarian, symbolic and mixed. So he's really into exchange. He's also into nearly everything else – he has published respectable work in psychology, health behaviour, and even statistics. A bit of a polymath, our Richard.

Not everybody agrees with Bagozzi about the exchange thing (see Chapter 5) but the concepts he espouses are at least interesting, and at most controversial.

Peter Doyle

In 2000, Peter Doyle published a seminal book entitled *Value-based Marketing*, in which he shot a big hole in the idea of customer centrality. The aim of the book was to redefine the role of marketing and clarify how its success (or otherwise) should be measured. His argument was that marketing has not been integrated with the modern concept of value creation: it is still caught up in the profit-making paradigm, which is not actually what companies do; in the main, companies are focused on maximizing shareholder value.

Doyle gave numerous examples of companies which had succeeded not through exceptional consumer value, but through creating and providing exceptional value to other stakeholders. He pointed out that only 12 chief executives of the UK's top 100 companies had any marketing experience, and 43 per cent of UK companies had no marketing representation on the Board. Doyle attributes this to a failure of marketers to take on board the concept of shareholder value, which is (in general) the main preoccupation of boards of directors. In fact, Doyle regards this as the primary obligation of directors, in which assertion he is largely in agreement with company law: directors are in fact under a primary obligation to look after shareholders' money, not to go oiling round the customers.

This leads on to the idea that marketing is, in fact, a means to an end: providing customer value is only a stage in the process of increasing shareholder value.

The book *Value-based Marketing* is, in my opinion, a landmark in marketing thinking. The ideas in it are only semi-developed, however, because they have not really been debated by marketers or by anybody else much. Sadly, Peter Doyle died recently at a relatively young age, so he has not had the opportunity to develop his ideas further, but I have the feeling that some bright young academic will come along any minute and pick up the dropped baton.

Wroe Alderson

Wroe Alderson is a semi-forgotten guru of marketing. You may never hear his name in a lecture, or read about him in a current marketing textbook, but he probably contributed more to marketing thought in the 1940s, 1950s and 1960s than anyone else.

Alderson contributed the basic idea of heterogeneity of both supply and demand. This is the idea that products differ from each other, as do consumers, and therefore direct competition between products is not the aim of marketing. Rather it is the development of niches. The heterogeneity of demand led to the concept of segmentation.

He also contributed the idea that firms are ecological systems that change and grow as circumstances dictate. This is part of the foundation of modern marketing strategy thinking. One of my favourite Wroe Alderson contributions, though, is the view of intermediaries, such as retailers and wholesalers, in sorting goods and assembling one-stop portfolios. This insight shows us that intermediaries are actually performing useful functions, so that cutting out the middle man is likely to increase costs rather than reduce them.

Wroe Alderson was from a Quaker background, and was known as a modest man. He was also famous for his almost incomprehensible writing style (Morris Holbrook said: 'Here was a writer who could not express himself clearly to save his soul'). But even this aspect of the man is open to debate. Stephen Brown (see above) describes him as a gifted literary stylist whose reputation is partly attributable to his writing style. This may well be true – obscurity is often associated with erudition, and far too many academics have managed to establish a wonderful reputation simply because no one can understand enough of what they are saying in order to make an effective criticism. This is not the case with Wroe Alderson. Even after hacking one's way through the syntax, the underlying thoughts are the basic building-blocks of modern marketing.

In 2006 the *European Business Review* published a special edition in which academics were asked to contribute articles which show how modern marketing has built on Alderson's work. Alderson's attempts to develop a unified theory of marketing, and his suggestions for doing so, have provided a fertile ground for 'blue sky' researchers and thinkers ever since. Ironic, really, since Alderson was a firm believer in the idea that marketing should be practical first, and theoretical second.

miscellaneous gurus

In a chapter of this nature it is inevitable that I will leave out somebody's favourite guru. Any list of marketing gurus suffers from the same weakness as any list of Top Footballers of All Time, or Top Bands Ever: it is a personal, subjective list. Some other names you will come across are (in no particular order):

Mike Saren: A former professor at Strathclyde (the Shangri La for British marketers), Mike is currently at Leicester where he thinks about critical marketing. He is best known for being editor of the *Journal of Marketing Theory*, which publishes many of the more 'blue sky' ideas on, er, marketing theory.

Michael Baker: Michael is Emeritus Professor of Marketing at Strathclyde, which means basically he has retired from the university but they still want his name on the books. He is a modest man who hates being described as a guru, so he will probably never speak to me again, but he has done more than any other British academic to develop marketing as an academic subject.

Nigel Piercy: A sometimes controversial character, Nigel is a marketing strategist who has managed to produce a strong output of serious research papers alongside some top-selling airport bookshop strategy guides. One of my favourite Piercy ideas is what he calls SPOTS, which stands for Strategic Plan On The Shelf. It refers to the way managers typically produce a gorgeous strategic plan which, after it has been shown to the bank manager or the shareholders, is placed neatly on the shelf and never opened again.

Martin Evans: Martin is best known these days for his work on direct marketing, and in particular database marketing. He has been fretting about privacy issues in database marketing since at least 1994, and he coined the memorable phrase 'Domesday Marketing' to describe the complete cataloguing of individuals through combining databases. Scary stuff – read his papers!

Michael Porter: Though he is not a marketer, Michael Porter's influence on marketing strategy has been very considerable. His Five Forces Theory of competition, his four basic competitive strategies, and his analysis of the value chain have all been seized on by marketers as if he were one of our own. In fact, his first degree was in engineering, and his PhD was in economics. So there you go – marketing is not as blinkered as some people would have you believe.

to conclude

Becoming defined as a guru is not all that simple. First, you need to have something important and preferably profound to say. Secondly, you need to be able to express it clearly and concisely – a problem which Wroe Alderson in particular had trouble with, as has Philip Kotler. Thirdly, you need to be in the right place at the right time, and also in the right journals at the right time.

Gurus are supposed to speak in obscure aphorisms, and many journals only seem to accept papers written in obscure language, so the pressure is on. Writing a couple of interesting textbooks, or an airport bookshop guide to marketing, is not enough to raise you to the peerage.

The existence of gurus seems to lend weight to the idea that marketing is a real science, though, and that was certainly the main thrust of Wroe Alderson's thinking, and Shelby Hunt later on. The next chapter considers the arguments surrounding the key concepts of marketing – the arguments our gurus helped to create and perpetuate.

4

Marketing Concepts and Contexts

One of the odd things about studying marketing is that the concepts are simple, in fact obvious, but seem to be extremely difficult to put into practice. For example, customer centrality is a no-brainer. If we don't look after our customers, someone else will. If we expect people to give us their money, we have to look after them properly. And so forth. Putting the customers first is so obvious it scarcely needs stating – so where's the problem?

The trouble is, it's hard to do in the real world. For a start, other people have needs too: the employees, the other people who are affected by the company and its products (such as neighbours), the shareholders (who, after all, own the business) and last but not least the managers. I have spent most of my working life running businesses, and I have never been able to be customer-centred: my employees and the bank manager always seemed to have more to say about it than I did, or even the customers did. Of course, we always spoke nicely to the customers and tried to look after them, but centre the business around them? Not on your life!

Let's think about the true implications of customer centrality for a moment. Do the customers get the best parking space in the car park? No. This is usually reserved for the managing director. Do the customers get invited to the Christmas party? No. This is usually for staff only (perhaps just as well). When we report the company's results, do the customers typically figure in the report? Not often – unless they are big and important and the sales manager wants to show the shareholders that he or she is doing his or her job. Annual results are always couched in financial terms, not in terms of customer loyalty, spend per customer, market penetration, customer satisfaction, and so forth.

The same problem of being obvious yet difficult to implement is true of other marketing concepts. Take the marketing mix, for example.

if I knew you were coming I'd have baked a cake

Marketers are supposedly acting like chefs, mixing various ingredients (product, price, place and promotion, for example) in the right proportions to ensure a good outcome in terms of customer satisfaction, profit and so forth. So far so good. The problem lies in defining the ingredients correctly, and categorizing them appropriately. For example, price is quite clearly decided by the customer (whatever the marketers might think). If a price is too high, customers simply will not pay it – they will go elsewhere. If the price is too low, customers will buy up all of the cheap version of the product and will then be forced to buy the more expensive version until the price becomes totally unacceptable. Since marketers can almost always increase sales by dropping the price, money-off sales promotions are used all the time, which means that price has become a promotional tool. The same is true of most of the mix ingredients: there are so many overlaps that it does not seem realistic to continue to pigeonhole marketing activities in this arbitrary way.

Another criticism of the marketing mix approach is that it implies that we are doing something to consumers, rather than doing something for them. The mix is almost always interpreted as being something which is applied to the market in order to win profits – so it might be seen to be in conflict with customer centrality, simply because the customer is seen to be passive in the process, just waiting to be presented with a beautifully-baked combination of mix ingredients. The mix has also been criticized for emphasizing structure over process (Kent, 1986) and, as a managerial approach, placing the main responsibility on the marketing department rather than encouraging marketing thinking to permeate the whole organization, as Drucker recommended. The main reason I am suspicious of the marketing mix approach is that it is far too simplistic, and is in any case forty years out of date. We have a great many more than four ingredients to play with. We also keep inventing new ones which do not fit the existing model. In 1960, when McCarthy presented the four Ps to an eager world, there were no printed T-shirts, no interactive TV broadcasts, no personal computers (let alone the Internet), no ambient advertising, no international satellite or even cable TV, and (heaven forefend) no mobile telephones. The most sophisticated direct marketing approach was brush salesmen knocking on housewives' doors during the day, and the only commercial radio available in the UK was Radio Luxembourg, which could only be received at night and which faded in and out so much that radio engineers referred to skip-fade as 'Luxembourg effect'. In other words, we were in the Dark Ages and grateful for anything.

In fact, come to think of it, one of the odd aspects of such a young discipline as marketing is that many of the models we use are seriously out of date. Why this should be so is hard to say. Perhaps we don't like to let go of an idea, or perhaps we can't be bothered to revisit the research which produced the idea (there is evidence that very few research exercises in marketing are duplication research, whereas duplication studies form the majority of research in the physical sciences). There is, of course, an inherent inertia caused by the teaching process: textbook writers are expected to include the received wisdom, otherwise lecturers will not recommend the books and publishers will therefore not publish them, so the same ideas keep on being repeated year after year. As textbook writers, we have a responsibility to engineer change by increment – a good textbook should be about 20 per cent new stuff, and 80 per cent old hat, so eventually we should be able to replace some of the old ideas. To be fair, the new ideas should also be replaced in their turn – we shouldn't pretend that marketing academics are always right, any more than any other academics. What we propose as current theory is unlikely to be perfect, it is simply the best we have at present.

The managerial framework implied by the marketing mix idea assumes that the firm is independent of its environment (Anderson and Soderlund, 1988). This may have been true in 1960 (although frankly I doubt it) but it certainly is not true in the twenty-first century, when firms are locked into value chains. Firms nowadays cannot control their environment, and it would be damaging to try to do so given the delicate nature of business relationships. Firms are not concerned with owning or controlling all their sources of supply and distribution, but rather are concerned with maintaining effective and flexible relationships to deal with an unstable world. Mix management assumes that the buyers and sellers are separate, adversarial entities rather than partners in a value chain, and it also assumes that markets are homogeneous and stable, which they emphatically are not.

The main advantage of the four P (or seven P or 13 P) list is that it makes it easy to structure a marketing course or a textbook. I am somewhat guilty of this myself: simplifying the world so that first-year undergraduates can get their heads round it is an occupational hazard of teaching in higher education. This is despite the frustration and annoyance I felt when, at age 16, I was told by my chemistry teacher that the orbits of electrons are not neat circles as we had been told at O-level (GCSE to you), but were in fact figures-of-eight, ellipsoids, or even (oh, crikey) wavicles rather than actual particles. I was annoyed at having to un-learn something which had taken me some time to grasp in the first place, and I felt I had been lied to. In which case, perhaps we should move away from basing everything on an outmoded and inaccurate model – otherwise I am as guilty of fooling my public as was my chemistry teacher.

that old bar-X brand

Branding is regarded as the focus of marketing activities – the brand is supposed to have a personality. This means that people can relate to it, learn to love it, and feel that they want to share their lives with it. Surprisingly, this type of connection actually happens. After all, people often have pet names for their cars, and we all talk to inanimate objects sometimes (usually in a pleading or threatening tone, using phrases such as 'Please get me home!'

or 'Start, you b&*%^*£!'). In fact, some interesting research conducted by a commercial market research company showed that people often think of their brand of coffee as a friend, and think of their bank as an acquaintance at best and an enemy at worst. Worrying news for the financial services industry, but logical in its way – coffee gets you through times with no money better than money gets you through times with no coffee. Actually, getting the brand to have a recognizable personality is not at all easy. Then, people relate to some brands and not to others, and what's more they seem to relate to inanimate brands better than they do to brands such as banks, which are after all made of people.

Branding goes back hundreds of years, of course. It has its roots in the days of cattle farming, when farmers would burn a mark on to their cattle to prove ownership. Later on, when manufacturing got under way, brands showed that the product had come from a particular manufacturer, and so were a sign of quality. Promoting the brand naturally led to the idea of focusing marketing efforts through the brand, and eventually to developing a brand persona. The Pear's Soap idea of buying Millais' painting, 'Bubbles', and asking the artist to add a bar of Pear's Soap to it in order to create an advertising poster eventually led to the company using very young children as the basis of their advertising. Going even further, for over forty years the company ran a Miss Pears beauty competition for pre-teen girls. This would be a somewhat controversial promotional device nowadays, but it was not seen as anything unusual in the 1950s when it started. Other brand personalities have been developed in a more abstract form. Honda used the persona 'rugby player in a dinner suit' to convey the style of the Honda Civic to the hundreds of designers, engineers and marketers who worked on its development. The brand can be seen as a lens through which marketers focus their efforts, or, looked at from the other direction, the brand is the lens through which the customers can see the product and the company in all their glory.

The purpose of the brand is to generate involvement, another key concept in consumer behaviour. Involvement is about falling in love with the product – which is not entirely unknown. One can readily imagine that someone might place great importance on buying the right brand. A hundred years ago people defined themselves by what they produced, but in the twenty-first century people define themselves by what they consume. Sometimes involvement serves a practical purpose. As a pilot, I would probably rate the reliability of a brand of aero engine as being an important issue, and I would certainly be interested in the safety aspects of the airframe. If the engine stops at 10,000 feet there is plenty of time to glide in for a forced landing; if the wings fall off there is really not a lot one can do to get down safely. In other cases involvement is about emotional issues: one looks cool in Diesel jeans, one looks distinctly uncool in Tesco's Value jeans.

The concept of the brand as the focus, and focusing device, for marketing activities is extremely useful. At the same time, it provides us with one of the great debates of business life, which is the measurement of brand equity. Valuing brands is a major issue for marketers, because they are continually up against a battle for budgets. Finance directors typically want to see a return on any expenditure, so they will tend to ask awkward questions such as 'If we run this £2 million advertising campaign, how much extra revenue will it generate?' This is the kind of direct question that marketers find difficult to answer, since they have been brought up to believe that you can't measure a communications action with a market outcome.

What was that again?

You can't measure a communications action with a market outcome. You can test the effectiveness of a campaign which was intended to raise public awareness of the brand by checking whether more people know about the brand after the campaign was run than knew about the brand before the campaign was run. You can check whether people regard the product better now than they did before. You can check whether they now understand your USP (or Unique Selling Proposition, for those of you who are new to marketing-speak) better now than they did before. What you can't do is be sure that the increase in sales (or

decrease, or lack of movement) can be attributed to your communications because there are too many other factors which might
have intervened in the process.

The result is that the marketing manager now tries to explain
why the success or otherwise of the campaign cannot be assessed in
those terms. This is impossible to do, because finance directors have
been brought up with the not-unreasonable view that any money
paid out on behalf of the firm should be expected to come back in,
bringing its friends with it – otherwise the company will disappear.
The answer, from the marketer's viewpoint, is to suggest that any
major promotional expenditure is an *investment in the brand's
equity* and can be expected to generate an income stream for years
to come. The finance director now can nod sagely, and when the
marketing manager suggests that promotional expenditure should
be moved from the profit-and-loss account to the balance sheet, he
or she is ready to agree, subject to knowing how big the income
stream will be.

To digress for a moment into the realms of financial account-
ing: the company can be valued in three ways. First, the firm can
be valued in terms of its physical assets – plant, machinery,
premises, cash in the bank, debts owed to it, and so forth. This
somewhat undervalues the firm, because it usually has a greater
value which includes surpluses included under 'good will'. This is
a catch-all category accountants use to make the books balance.
The goodwill provides us with our second valuation. Thirdly, the
firm is valued by its shareholders, based on what the shares sell
for. This valuation is determined by the stock market, based on
what the shareholders feel about holding shares in the company,
a feeling which is based as much on the gut as on the performance
of the shares.

This means that the marketers are substantially right in their
assertion about the value of the brand. Firms such as Nike and
Coca-Cola have little or no physical assets – very little plant and
equipment, few or no factories, small office space, and so forth.
Virtually everything they sell is produced under licence or under
contract, and the main function of the company is to manage the

brand. Companies like these are valued by the stock market in terms of their profitability and their security (who could imagine that Coca-Cola could go broke, or could even lose money?), not in terms of their physical assets, so it makes perfect sense to ensure that the brand is well known and popular.

Determining how much a specific campaign will add to the value of the company is difficult, to say the least, because sometimes campaigns backfire and actually reduce the value of the firm, but what we do know for certain is that companies which do not invest in their marketing will disappear without trace. What we also know is that companies which establish their brands well in the minds of both consumers and potential investors raise the value of their companies on the stock market. From the viewpoint of the company directors this can only be a good thing – it discharges their legal obligation to protect shareholders' interests, and (more importantly) it protects the company from being taken over, and therefore allows the directors to carry on having fun.

talk to me!

In 1968 I left home and school (at the age of sixteen) to join the Merchant Navy as a radio officer. Naturally, we were taught communication theory, and at the time the main theory was the Schramm model (Schramm, 1948). This model says that, for communication to be effective, there must be a transmitter, a receiver, a medium for communication, and some kind of intelligence (a message, in other words). The communication might be distorted by noise or interference, but the basic model would still apply. Later on Schramm added the idea that there should also be feedback, and that there should be a commonality of fields of experience for the transmitter and the receiver, at least to the extent of sharing a common language. As trainee radio officers our common language was Morse code, of course. When I joined my first ship I became painfully aware of the effects of noise and interference – I scarcely managed to receive a single message correctly for the first month I was at sea, and I only coped after that by buying a tape recorder in Singapore and taping all the messages. This saved me the embarrassment of continually asking the shore stations to repeat the message.

Marketing communications theory has been dominated for over fifty years by the Schramm model of communications. I have taught this model, and it appears in my books, so I have to accept my share of the blame, but it seems to me that the model is fatally flawed in one respect: people are not radios.

People think about what they hear and read, and they do not ask advertisers to repeat the message. They also have a habit of adding the message to what they already know, and thus 'distorting' the message even further.

So why do we still cling to Schramm like a shipwrecked sailor to a lifebelt? I suspect because it is easy to teach and to understand. Maybe I'm just being cynical, though.

you can't choose your relations

Getting consumers to be involved with the brand is the Holy Grail of marketing – yet another example of a marketing concept which is easy to state but hard to implement. The involved consumer is the loyal consumer, which is why companies keep looking to develop relationships with their customers. Relationship marketing was the buzz word of the 1990s and is still buzzing now. The reason we want to establish relationships is that it is cheaper to keep an existing customer than it is to find a new one (although the research which backs this up is somewhat elusive). Most textbooks suggest that it is five times cheaper to keep a customer than to gain a new one, and so companies are almost fawning over their customers to the point where it becomes embarrassing for all concerned. The 'courtesy' phone call which is a euphemism for telephone selling, the endless stream of mailings to people who are already customers, the TV advertising assuring people that existing customers will be offered the same benefits as new customers, and of course the ubiquitous loyalty cards are all aimed at customer retention. In fact, of course, all the company has to do is produce products that work, and services that satisfy for people to stay on board.

The evidence is that the relationship marketing process works much better in business-to-business markets than in business-to-consumer markets. This is almost certainly because the needs of a business change much more slowly than the needs of an individual. Businesses make the same basic things year after year, they use the same raw materials, operate the same systems, and do not (in general terms) grow old and die. There are many businesses which are over a hundred years old, still producing much the same products, and still bidding fair to become two hundred years old or more. People last about seventy to eighty years, and for a lot of this time they are not of much interest economically, either because they are too young or because they are too old or because they do not have much money. Relationship marketing, therefore, is yet another simple concept which is nigh impossible to apply in practice.

Other reasons for the greater success of relationship marketing in business to business are not hard to guess – business buyers find it much easier and more advantageous to continue to buy from the same supplier rather than shift to a new one. Professional buyers are in a difficult position because they need to make purchases, but they are spending other people's money and might have to account for wrong decisions. People buying for themselves might simply discard purchases which haven't worked out, but business buyers have to live with their mistakes. Naturally this makes them a bit gun-shy about switching suppliers, so there is a premium placed on establishing an 'approved supplier' list.

From the supplier's viewpoint, nothing could be better than being on the approved supplier list, because it means everyone can go back to sleep, only waking up long enough to ensure that there is 'business as usual' at the customer's premises. On the other hand, in business-to-consumer markets, suppliers need to be much more circumspect and generally on the ball because customers can switch suppliers so much more easily.

Establishing good relationships has been compared to courtship and marriage (see Theodore Levitt's section in Chapter 3). Marriage is generally regarded as a relationship of equals, though, and most business relationships are unlikely to be very equal. One or other partner almost always has the upper hand, either because of size and buying power or because there are many competing suppliers. Business relationships are much more akin to seduction, bigamy, or worse. Another problem is that relationship marketing still concentrates on dyadic relationships – one seller, one buyer. This is all well and good, except that the real world isn't like that. Most firms have many suppliers and even more customers, so it is impossible to develop the kind of close relationship one has with one's spouse. In a marriage, one adapts what one does to fit the needs of the other person (the perfect marketing approach, in fact) but where would we start to adapt everything we do when we are dealing with scores, hundreds, or even thousands of customers? We are forced to offer a standard response, or even a range of standard responses, which necessarily are less than perfect.

Another aspect of relationship marketing which wants watching is the cost of divorce. The cost of switching suppliers is generally not as high as the cost of finding new customers, so again the relationship is unlikely to be one of equals. Recently, I took out a credit card because they offered me an interest-free six months. I used the money to make a major purchase, knowing that I had a royalty cheque due in before the six months was up and I could pay off the card and cancel it. In effect, I was bringing the purchase forward by six months – instant gratification at the expense of the finance company. After I cancelled the card and paid it off, I had a very nice phone call from the credit card company begging me to reconsider – even though I had, in effect, cheated them out of around £500 in interest payments. Why do they do this? Why do they act like a lovesick teenager, hanging around outside the ex-girlfriend's house after being dumped? I suspect it is because they have been on a customer retention course, and have not realized that some customers are not worth having. In my case, I was not really a customer at all – I never paid them anything.

From a consumer's viewpoint, many companies are acting more like stalkers than like lovers. Some firms, especially credit card companies and similar financial services companies, are apt to jump out from behind the bushes when you least expect them, all in the name of customer retention.

All of these criticisms have been levelled at relationship marketing theory. Establishing long-term relationships is known to be a good thing, but in practice it seems to be more elusive than most firms expect.

needs and wants

Part of the problem in establishing relationships with many different customers is that people differ in their needs and wants. Defining what is a need and what is a want is one of the knotty problems in studying marketing because marketers use specific definitions for these words which do not, in my experience, accord with the definitions used by most people.

A need is, for marketers, a perceived lack of something. This means that, not only do we not have something, but we know we don't have it and we think this is a missing factor in our lives. The argument goes that people did not need houses when we lived in caves, because we had perfectly good accommodation, except for the family of bears living in the cave next door. Once the semi-detached house was invented, living in a cave would have certainly been perceived as lacking in amenities and the semi would become a need – even allowing for the neighbours. My favourite example of this is the natives of Tierra del Fuego, a group of islands at the southernmost tip of South America. These hunter-gatherers lived in an extremely harsh climate. Tierra del Fuego is the southernmost tip of the continent, and has a climate like Norway, with plenty of snow in the winter, yet the Tierra del Fuegans (the Yamana tribe) had not invented clothing (well, you can't think of everything). They did wear loincloths for the purposes of modesty, but in all other respects they went about their daily tasks dressed mainly in their own skins, and animal grease. The Yamana had, however, invented fire, so they could light big bonfires in the winter and stand around them to keep warm, and also to cook penguins, which were a large part of their diet. When Magellan sailed past the islands on 21 October 1520 he saw the big fires and called the country Land of the Fire – Tierra del Fuego. Since this was the southern hemisphere, October is spring so the fires were probably somewhat less than they would have been in July or August, but no doubt it was still a bit on the fresh side.

Once the Yamana were introduced to European ways, they took to wearing clothes and probably felt pretty silly for not having thought of the idea for themselves. The point is that they did not have a need for clothing until they saw that it existed, and they could see the advantages. They did need fire, so they discovered it and enjoyed having it: having fire meant that they did not need clothes. In common with most other aborigine tribes, they did not survive contact with Europeans and quickly succumbed to unfamiliar diseases, famine due to the penguins moving out, and of course being shot by European farmers. Colonists therefore achieved in about twenty years what the harsh climate and lack of clothing had failed to achieve in a thousand years – the extinction of the Yamana.

Obviously most of us have similar needs in some respects – we all need to eat, to drink, and to live indoors (at least in Northern Europe we do). We also need to have friends, to have work that interests us and which provides money, and to have pleasurable things in our lives such as artworks and music. There have been many attempts to classify human needs, culminating in the most widely taught and widely quoted model, Maslow's 'Hierarchy of Needs'. If you haven't seen this yet, believe me, you will. Maslow first published his model in 1954, and it purports to show that people have needs in common, and that the needs are met in a set sequence (at least, broadly speaking). At the bottom of the hierarchy are survival needs: food, shelter, water. Next up are security needs, ensuring that the supply of survival products will continue unabated. Above this level we find the belonging needs and the esteem needs. These are about being a respected member of the group. Further up again are aesthetic needs – the artworks and music mentioned earlier. Finally, at the very top is self-actualization, the point at which our lucky individual has everything he or she wants, and can indulge in doing things just for the hell of it (Maslow, 1954). When Sir James Goldsmith sold up his successful food conglomerate and used the money to buy a rain forest he was self-actualizing. When someone retires from work and spends his every waking moment trying to grow the largest vegetable marrow in the village he is self-actualizing. When a film star chooses to act in a movie which promotes a good cause, but which will never be box-office, he or she is self-actualizing.

In fact, Maslow's hierarchy has more holes in it than a swiss cheese. For one thing, it ignores artists starving in garrets. These people are obviously more concerned either with self-actualizing or with esteem needs than they are with survival needs. For another thing, it ignores people who simply don't care what other people think of them. For a third thing, people often move from one sort of need to another in the course of a day, wanting esteem in work, and seeking to belong at a nightclub, for example. Finally, the distinction between the various categories of need is an artificial one. People do not eat to survive (at least in industrial countries there is little need to), they eat for pleasure (aesthetic needs) or for esteem needs (having friends round for dinner, or going to a restaurant), or for self-actualization needs (losing weight, becoming a better cook, training for the marathon, etc.). I have a personal dislike of Maslow's hierarchy: apart from the fact that his estate charges $75 permission fee for reproducing the diagram in a book, Maslow drew it as a pyramid and then put 'self-actualization' in the topmost, and therefore smallest, box. This makes the diagram difficult to draw on a whiteboard.

Marketers spend much of their time encouraging people to think about their needs, and the rest of their time suggesting to them that they can satisfy those needs by buying a specific product. The Yamana, mentioned earlier, developed a need for clothing once they had seen it. If some enterprising time-travelling marketer had turned up with a container full of North Face heavy-weather clothing, he or she would have sold out in minutes.

Wants are defined as specific satisfiers for needs. In Introduction to Marketing Lecture One we always have to explain this definition, because most people define 'need' as being something that is essential to life, and 'want' as something which is not essential, but which might be considered to be a luxury item. Using definitions which differ radically from those in common usage is not confined to marketers, of course, and in fact marketing is a relatively jargon-free discipline compared with many real sciences, but this is one that causes us particular difficulty, often taking up most of a tutorial session. As a definition, though, it does have advantages. It avoids the problem of deciding what is essential and what is not (this is, after all, subjective), and it is neat and snappy. It follows on neatly from the definition of need, which is also subjective.

However, because people have differing needs, marketers need to think about how they are going to approach the market. Simply plugging the product at every opportunity to as many people as possible is not the way forward. Few firms would have the resources to do this, and even in those which do, the marketing manager is extremely unlikely to be handed a blank cheque and be told to go out and spend it. Working within a budget means being choosy about where the money is spent, and this in turn means deciding which customers are worth having and which are not. This leads us neatly on to segmentation and targeting, two activities which are so closely linked they are usually taught in one lecture and are nearly always in the same chapter of the textbook.

all together now: buy something!

The segmentation concept is again very simple and obvious to state: the idea of dividing the potential market into groups of people with similar needs and devoting the firm's limited resources to supplying the needs of only a few of the groups makes perfect sense. In segmentation, we are seeking to categorize people according to their needs. The implementation problem here is that it means pigeonholing people, perhaps putting them in with others with whom they do not easily fit. Also, people do not necessarily stay in their segments. They change their needs, change their ideas, change their circumstances and consequently they move out of the pigeonhole. Other people may move in to take their places, of course, but we therefore need to consider a market segment as a fluid thing, not as something which is always composed of specific individuals. This is a point which often eludes marketers.

The other problem with segmentation is that it means deciding which customers we don't want to do business with. In some cases this is because they are just too much trouble, too expensive to deal with, or maybe we just can't meet their needs. In practice, though, are we really going to turn away people who don't fit the segment? Maybe – if they are real troublemakers! Repelling the undesirables is as much of a challenge as attracting the target segment – and again, this is a point which is often overlooked.

Imagine, for example, a pub in a rough area of the city. At one table we see a bunch of tough guys, drinking and swearing and singing rude songs. At the next table we have a little old lady and gentleman trying to enjoy a quiet drink. Finally, the old gentleman goes to the pub landlord and asks him to intervene – the loutish behaviour at the next table is upsetting his wife. 'Fine', says the landlord, 'Finish your drinks and get out. We don't want your sort here.'

'But I'm not the one causing the trouble!', protests the old man.

'No, but they're going to spend £100 and more in here tonight, and you're going to sit there all night with two halves of lager. I need them, I don't need you!'

Reasonable behaviour? But that's what segmentation is all about! Deciding who are the undesirables is for the marketing manager to decide, and it will be decided on profitability, or strategic necessity, or competitive advantage, or for any one of a dozen reasons which have nothing to do with the welfare of the customer.

Which leads us back to the main concept of marketing – customer centrality. Customer centrality is not about doing the customers a drop of good. Marketers are not Mother Teresa. Customer centrality is about meeting corporate objectives by helping customers reach their objectives. The corporate objective

might be sales, it might be profits, it might be competitive positioning, it might be improving the image of the company's directors, it
might be growth, it might simply be survival in an increasingly dangerous corporate shark pool. Whatever the objectives, customers are
going to be seen as the source of success.

Marketers therefore have a single touchstone for solving business problems. Like a one-trick pony, marketers always begin by
looking at the customer. If we understand the needs, drives, decision-
making processes, and general objectives of the customers, we
have a very good chance of being able to manage the exchange
process to our own advantage. Of course, people are not as stupid
as all that, so we will have to ensure that the exchange is to their
advantage as well. So how can we both end up better off as the
result of the exchange?

managing exchange: relationships, segments, individuals, and leaky buckets

There is an old saying – fair exchange is no robbery. I remember
having that proverb quoted at me in primary school, after a so-
called 'friend' had exchanged my rare and valuable Indian rupee
piece for his commonplace French franc. There had been an
exchange all right – but it was hardly fair, since I was dissatisfied
with the outcome. He, on the other hand, went away well pleased
with himself and has no doubt founded an excellent business career
on this early experience. However, unless he is working for the tax
authorities he will have to have learned to give a reasonable
exchange for his goods – there is a difference between business and
larceny.

The difference lies in the differing values people place on
goods. For one person, a cream cake is much more desirable than
a chicken sandwich, whereas the reverse might be true of another
person. For the chicken-sandwich fancier who has been given a
cream cake, an exchange with the cream-cake lover would be
advantageous. Likewise, the cream-caker lumbered with a surplus
chicken sandwich might also want to exchange. This is a simple

but obvious example. Since we cannot be forever looking for someone who has something we want in order to exchange for something we don't want, we use money as the medium of exchange. We now find that the sandwich shop has a surplus of both cream cakes and sandwiches, and a proprietor who would much rather end the day with a till full of money than with a shop full of sandwiches. Likewise, we have a large group of customers who would rather have a stomach full of sandwiches (or cream cakes) than a pocket full of money. The problem for the proprietor lies in determining how many sandwiches and cream cakes to make each day, which is of course a marketing problem since he or she will have to decide what the potential demand might be, and what kinds of sandwich the customers would like to buy. After all, if the anchovy and custard sandwiches were not a success, people will go to another sandwich shop.

You may recall a discussion of the Edgeworth Box model (kindly contributed by economists Edgeworth and Pareto) in Chapter 1. The Edgeworth Box operationalizes this fairly obvious idea, and shows us the mechanisms by which exchange is negotiated.

The basis of the exchange is therefore always a disparity in how people judge value. This is why it is misleading to talk about 'the consumer' as if consumers are all the same. Consumers differ a great deal from each other. They are a lot like people in that respect. What segmentation is intended to achieve is finding people whose needs are similar, and targeting is about choosing which groups to go for, and how to go about it.

Targeting follows on naturally from segmentation, but is also not always easy to do in practice. For example, we might have identified the correct segments of the market, but somebody else much bigger and more powerful is already meeting the needs of the most attractive segments. This makes the segment less attractive, rather as if the town tough guy has just sat down in the chair by the pub fire, thus making the other chairs near the fire less attractive. One is then faced with the unenviable decision as to whether to risk the wrath of the tough guy (who, after all, may be feeling benevolent this evening after all) or finding somewhere colder to sit. Luring an attractive segment away from a large competitor could be dangerous, but if it works, it could also be very lucrative. What most smaller companies do, though, is look for a smaller, less attractive segment which the big players do not much care about. Feeding on the crumbs, the small firm hopes to survive and grow strong enough to stand up to the bullies.

The difficulty, as always, is that companies can convey their messages to individuals or groups without too much difficulty, but those individuals may move out of the group as their needs change. For example, any parent will tell you how wonderful Calpol is. For those of you who are not parents, Calpol is made by Pfizer, and is a pain-killer for children and babies. A baby with a headache, stomach ache, muscle pain, bruise, nappy rash or you-name-it does not have the concept of allowing its parents to sleep at night. Calpol has saved many a marriage by simply getting the baby off to sleep. In my own case, I am no longer in the market for Calpol, since my children are grown up but not yet parents themselves. The only time I buy it is if I have friends who are first-time parents, and who perhaps do not know of the miraculous powers of Calpol. (Incidentally, the strap line for Calpol is 'If you've got kids, you'll understand'.) Therefore, as a customer for Calpol I have moved out of the target group, and have not yet moved back in. The same is true for any parent as their children grow up.

This is the main problem for relationship marketing in consumer markets. The idea behind relationship marketing is to move away from focusing on the single transaction, and to move towards considering the 'lifetime value' of a customer. In the past, companies have followed the 'leaky bucket' approach identified by Ehrenberg. In Ehrenberg's world, each company has a bucket full of customers, but there are holes in the bucket and customers leak out. The typical response to this is to recruit new customers to replace them, whereas of course the sensible thing to do would be to fix the leaks (Ehrenberg, 1988). Earlier on I mentioned that it is cheaper to keep an existing customer than it is to recruit a new one, so companies seek to win customer loyalty. They do this in many ways: in consumer markets, firms reward loyalty by giving customers extra gifts or prizes for being regular shoppers. Firms also write to customers, telephone them, e-mail them with special offers or news of new products, give discounts to existing customers or trade-in deals for old products, and so on. In business-to-business markets firms try to co-ordinate their systems with the customer, supply services which the customer comes to rely on, and become involved in joint development of new products. All these activities tend to 'lock in' the customer company, although they make the divorce even more painful when it eventually happens.

In fact, relationship marketing is often compared to a marriage. The marriage analogy is usually credited to Theodore Levitt (see Chapter 3), a man who is normally a very clear thinker on marketing concepts in general. If you recall, Levitt suggests that companies 'court' customers, putting on their best face to attract the customers, and then establishing a closer and closer relationship until the customer cannot imagine life without the company and its products. Caroline Tynan of Nottingham University took a rather robust view of the marriage analogy, though. She says that it is often less a courtship than a seduction, and in some cases rape might be a more appropriate definition of what actually happens (Tynan, 1997).

but is it rational?

As we saw in Part 1 of this book, because consumers are people, they often act irrationally. The buying process is far from being a coldly logical activity. Early economists such as Adam Smith (see Chapter 1) thought that people would seek to maximize the benefit they obtained from their limited stock of money. This utility maximization model is still popular in many circles, although it has become somewhat bent out of shape as further research into people's drives and motivations is carried out. Smith believed that people would shop around for the best value for money, which has a certain amount of truth in it if we take account of all the factors which might affect the decision. For example, few people would shop around for a plumber if the pipes had burst and the house was flooded – they would simply grab the first plumber who was available to come and fix the leak. On the other hand, some people are quite happy to spend half a morning going from supermarket to market stall to corner shop trying to buy a cabbage for 2p a pound less. The thrill of getting a bargain outweighs the obvious fact that the individual would do better to go to work for a morning and earn enough to buy 50 cabbages. This sort of behaviour is most inconsiderate – it throws a very large spanner into the delicate structure of Smith's oh-so-obvious theory.

The emotional content of the purchasing decision is an important issue for marketers. Much of the influence exerted on consumers is developed through their emotions rather than through their rational faculties. Giving someone the idea that buying a particular car will make them appear successful (or sexy, or cool, or whatever) works much better than explaining the gear ratios or the potential lifespan of the clutch plates. In the longer term, getting the customer to buy next year's model may well depend on these practical issues, but attracting them in the first place is often a matter of emotion rather than logic.

Furthermore, people are affected by other non-rational issues. Hedonism is one such factor. The pleasurable aspects of owning a product may outweigh practical issues. For some people, having the latest version of a product is an advantage in and of itself. For others, having a product which looks nice, or is comfortable to use, or which makes a thrilling noise is the important issue. People are affected by what other people think – being respected for owning a specific product may be a lot more important than actually using the thing. Then again, looking a fool because of owning the *wrong* thing is also a powerful driver.

As we saw in Chapter 1, people's attitudes to things are composed of three separate factors: affect (which is what they feel), cognition (which is what they think) and conation (which is what they intend to do about it). These factors work together and should be compatible. If they are not, the individual will need to make a smart re-adjustment in attitude. This latter fact is what marketers use in order to change people's attitudes. By changing any one of the factors, the marketer forces a change of attitude. Of course, this is rather like throwing pieces of jigsaw into the air and hoping they will make a new picture when they land on the floor, but it's the best we can do with what we have at present.

Destabilizing an attitude by changing the emotional content was classified by some researchers called Petty and Caccioppo (1983) as the peripheral route. This implies that the attitude change comes in a roundabout way, via the scenic route – which in turn implies that there is something vaguely dishonest about it, as if we are manipulating consumers. The same researchers refer to the direct route, which means changing attitudes by appealing to cognition. This seems to imply the honest, forthright approach, appealing to the individual's knowledge, putting the case in a straightforward and logical way. This distinction is purely artificial. Since much of what people like about products is emotional, it is hardly unfair to appeal to emotions.

As we saw in Chapter 2, attitude can also be changed by changing the individual's conation. Telling someone that their planned behaviour is impossible (for example, because the product no longer exists) will lead to a re-think on the part of the individual. This might also become unethical in some contexts – the frequency with which Third World taxi drivers tell you that the hotel you want has closed down, burned down, or fallen down is almost as amazing as the coincidence by which their cousin has a hotel which might have a room free. On the other hand, an honest piece of information which tells the individual that the planned course of action will not be possible can be regarded as extremely helpful.

Changing attitudes requires a clear understanding of what makes people tick. This understanding comes from the behavioural sciences. As we saw in Chapter 2, the psychologists, sociologists and anthropologists have all contributed to our knowledge of why people buy things. As marketers, we try to use this information to nudge people towards buying one thing rather than another. It is almost impossible for us to make much difference to people's basic needs (the factors that generate drives and motivations). What we can do is affect what people want (the specific satisfiers for the needs). In other words, the received wisdom in marketing is that we cannot make someone hungry or thirsty, but we can suggest to them that they might enjoy a hamburger and a glass of beer. This may be how advertising works – we don't really know, or rather we can't agree.

Here are the arguments. The obvious (and therefore probably wrong, if the rest of marketing thought is anything to go by) mechanism is that we shout 'Buy Some Today!' as loud as we can and some people will go and buy some. Naturally, putting ideas into people's heads is probably helpful, and at least some people will go ahead and buy. However, a competing theory has emerged in recent years. Our friend Andrew Ehrenberg (he of the leaky bucket theory) surmises that, in fact, the people who 'buy some today' were already halfway to the shop and were simply nudged towards buying a specific brand (Ehrenberg, 1974).

I rather like this theory of Ehrenberg's, not least because I would not like to think that people are as easily manipulated as all that by marketers. Also, having been a practitioner in my time, I know that we aren't actually as clever as all that. We can't manipulate people as efficiently as the critics of marketing would have you believe. The 'Weak Theory of Advertising' covers the case nicely because it suggest that advertising only increases sales among those who were already almost there anyway. It nudges rather than pushes, reminds rather than persuades, and helps decisions rather than forces them.

never use a short word when a long one will do

To conclude, marketing academics have a knack of thinking up simple theories to explain how marketing works. Practitioners, on the other hand, have great difficulty in putting those theories into practice. There is always something else that gets in the way – inconsiderate consumers who make irrational decisions, or shareholders who unreasonably demand that the company they own should work for their benefit, or rascally employees who think their decent working conditions should come ahead of those whining, demanding, unreasonable consumers. In addition, marketing academics often act like oracles, giving their advice in obscure language and with much verbosity, so that practitioners grow impatient and hurl the journal into the fire before they get past the first paragraph or two. If academics simply jumped up and down saying 'Why don't they listen to me?' it wouldn't be so bad. Jumping up and down saying 'What is the rationale for inattention on the part of proponents of exchange management to the emerging paradigm of interpretivist research outcomes?' is far worse (actually, that would be a good title for a paper). Luckily, most academics teach, which means they have plenty of opportunity to show off what they know in front of classes of students who have no option but to listen if they are going to get good grades.

Of course, marketing is still a young discipline. We are still developing the theories, and if we get the level of understanding about consumers that physicists have about the strength of materials, we might really develop some good practice. Thirty years ago, the number of UK academics with a PhD in marketing could be counted on the fingers of one thumb – now there are hundreds of us. To get a PhD you have to find out something new, so we have obviously added something to the sum of human knowledge: if we're lucky, it will have been something useful.

Meanwhile we muddle along with what we have, and what we have is an economic life characterized by products which work, an unprecedented level of choice, the highest standard of living our species has ever had, and a richness of life experience such as our ancestors could only have dreamed of. So maybe we're doing something right after all. The next chapter will look at how much of this success is due to marketing.

Selling Marketing

5

Why Marketing
Doesn't Work

In 1953, Fred Pohl and C.M. Kornbluth published a remarkable book in which they foresaw a world in which marketers had become so proficient that they controlled everything. Government would consist of representatives of major corporations, creative writers would all be dragooned into writing copy, to the extent that literature and poetry withered on the vine, anthropologists and sociologists would be employed in creating whispering campaigns, rumours, and jokes which would mould opinion, and biochemists would create additives which would trigger cravings for particular foods, drinks or cigrattes. The book, *The Space Merchants,* was of course science fiction, but it played on the very real fears people had that marketing had become a black art, capable of brainwashing people into buying products they do not want. This is a view which is often espoused fifty years later, along with the view that marketing is also damaging to people and other living things.

Incidentally, Pohl and Kornbluth postulated that the great enemies of the marketers would be the Conservationists. Remember that the book was written in 1953 (or rather in 1951 – publishers do take their time), long before the ecological movement dragged itself off the ground. The lead character in the book, Mitch Courtney (an ad executive for Fowler Schocken Associates), eventually becomes converted to the Conservationist cause by seeing what life has become for the underclass enslaved by the ad agencies. But I won't spoil the ending for you.

It is the nature of human beings that not everyone thinks that the black art view of marketing is a bad thing. Firms still hope that a wave of the market wand will transform the company's fortunes, make people buy stuff, and generally make everything all right. Some company directors have fleeting ethical twinges as a result of shamelessly exploiting their fellow man by letting the marketers loose on them, but most feel that it is for the long-term good of the firm. Academic marketers bleat ineffectually in the wings, trying to explain for the five hundredth time that marketing is about looking after customers, not brainwashing them, but people believe what they want to believe: getting the marketing right means shifting product, and not a lot else.

This may be why marketing doesn't work. The inevitable disappointment which sets in when the advertising budget has been spent and no new business has resulted is a sad thing to see, but advertising will only do what advertising can do. It can communicate fairly effectively, but it cannot force people to do things. We have yet to reach that level of sophistication, if we ever do, which is fairly unlikely.

The issue is whether or not adopting the marketing concept and loving the customers results in business success or not. There is considerable evidence to indicate that the answer is that it does not. An often-quoted fact is that the companies showcased in Peters and Waterman's book, *In Search of Excellence* (1982), all of which espoused the marketing concept (along with staff empowerment and low-pyramid organization structures), have lost market share or gone dramatically adrift in other ways since the book was published in 1982. Now, the pro-marketers say that there are many other factors involved, and those companies might have come unstuck for any number of reasons entirely unconnected with their marketing approach. But this doesn't sit well with the marketers' view that sticking to the marketing concept is the universal panacea for corporate success.

For those of us who study marketing somewhere other than at airport bookstalls, the awareness that marketing has not fulfilled its early promise despite having had at least fifty years to get its act together comes as no great surprise. We are well aware that we do not yet have a rigorous science of marketing, and even as an art it leaves a lot to be desired. Undismayed, we point to nuclear physics or astronautics to show that other young disciplines are in a similar state of disarray – and they are dealing with such simple matters as subatomic particles and (wait for it) rocket science. Marketing isn't rocket science. It's much more complex than that, because it deals with human beings, who are notoriously intractable, unpredictable, dangerous and difficult.

why academics disagree about marketing

We have to start from the viewpoint that marketing is itself derived from practice. We sometimes say that marketing derives from economics and behavioural science the same way engineering derives from physics and chemistry, but in fact even a brief look at the academic journals shows that this is substantially not the case. Marketing theory derives from marketing practice – academics almost always go out and see what practitioners are doing, or ask what consumers are doing, and codify their findings accordingly. Already we have a major divergence from the way engineering operates – in engineering, theory precedes practice.

Marketing academics probably justify this state of affairs to themselves on the basis that carrying out pure research into people's basic motivations is part of psychology or sociology, not part of marketing. This begs the question: where do we draw the line between marketing and everything else? And why do we need to?

Few people (with the possible exception of the Kotlerites) would take the view that everything in the world is marketing. Therefore, there must be a boundary between what is marketing and what is not if marketing is to be taken seriously as an academic subject. If a subject is to be accorded the status of a science, it needs to do two things: it needs to identify its unique distinguishing feature, in other words the field of study which is its own and nobody else's, and it needs to define its boundaries, its unique domain. However fuzzy the boundaries, there must be some point at which we say 'From here on, this is anthropology', or 'This is economics'. No one confuses economics with engineering (although apparently some people confuse anthropology with geology, according to an anthropologist acquaintance of mine).

Why does this matter, apart from offering us some esoteric theoretical perspective? Well, first, we need to direct the efforts of researchers. One would not want to fund a research programme in marketing and find that one had actually funded an anthropological or sociological study. Failure to focus effort will, ultimately, slow the development of the discipline. Without a clear definition of both core and boundaries, we are likely to witness an aimless wandering, and a preponderance of time wasted on fringe topics which have little or no connection with the core of the business.

At the same time, a failure to understand what marketing is and is not affects the ways in which practitioners manage the process. The extreme view here is Drucker's statement that 'A business has only one purpose – to create and keep a customer' (Drucker, 1954). He intended, I suppose, to indicate that responsibility for customer satisfaction must permeate the organization at all levels, but the statement can also be interpreted to mean that marketing managers have no separate role within the business. It is probably the case that most managers (whether marketers or not) have a fairly clear idea of what they are supposed to be doing each day, but turf wars are bound to result if the boundaries are not made very clear.

One view of marketing's boundaries was espoused by Bagozzi (see Chapter 3), building on a suggestion made by Anderson in the early 1960s. Bagozzi's view of marketing as exchange has caught on with marketers, and it is an appealing one: it is easy to understand, easy to apply as a yardstick, and, like most simple ideas, it is wrong. Marketing cannot be defined as being solely about exchange. Exchanges happen all the time. We exchange marriage vows, but that is not marketing. We exchange addresses with acquaintances, but that is not marketing either. We even exchange good behaviour for sweeties, and that is not marketing. Perhaps, then, marketing is about commercial exchanges, where money changes hands. The view of marketing as being concerned with profit has been the view of the UK's Chartered Institute of Marketing since its very beginnings. Its definition of marketing specifically mentions profit. This rules out the whole field of not-for-profit marketing which grew up around Kotler's ideas.

As mentioned in Chapter 3, Kotler and Levy sparked the debate with their 1969 paper, 'Broadening the Concept of Marketing'. This paper argued that marketing was applicable not only to businesses, but also to not-for-profit organizations, public sector organizations, and indeed many other non-business organizations such as clubs and charities. This view also had its adherents, and indeed not-for-profit marketing is widely taught (I teach it to social work managers in Germany, for example). For the concept to work, we have to suppose that all organizations have products and provide benefits to their 'customers', which means the people who hand over their money.

Hmmm.... We now have to perform some mental gymnastics to justify charitable contributions. What does a contributor gain from handing over a contribution to, say, Oxfam? The pleasure of giving, perhaps? A ticket of admission to the Kingdom of Heaven? Hard to say. Even less likely, we see the police force using advertising, public relations and even personal selling techniques on their 'customers'. Kotler and Levy therefore had to define 'consumer' very loosely for the proposed theory to stack up.

Again, societal marketing and not-for-profit marketing appealed to the average marketing professional because it provided a counter-argument to the black art theory. Marketers were able to say: 'Ah, yes, marketing may be a manipulative and unethical way of getting your money off you, but look at the good our charity campaign did.' In other words, manipulating people into going to the cinema or buying themselves something nice is bad, but harassing smokers to give up is okay.

In practice, applying the marketing mix across all organizations means stretching the basic definitions of its components beyond any reasonable limits. To argue that someone who gives up smoking as a result of an advertising campaign is a consumer, and that the Department of Health is a customer, is stretching things a bit. The short-term benefits of opening up new career opportunities by expanding marketing's role are undeniable, as is the neatness of the solution. The possibilities for getting rid of those bores who attack one at parties (on the basis that marketing is wicked) are simply an added bonus.

In 1969, Luck argued that marketing should restrict itself to those activities which ultimately result in a market transaction (Luck, 1969). Okay. Fine so far, but one cannot define a term by using the term itself. We still don't know what a market transaction is. Kotler would say that a charitable contribution, or a vote cast for a politician, is a market transaction, so Luck is still out of luck, if you will forgive the pun. Whether we broaden or narrow the definition of marketing is clearly still a vexed question.

Bartels (1976) argued that there are a number of basic problems which result from broadening the marketing domain. Specifically, these are as follows:

1. Marketing researchers would be diverted from important issues. Opening up new areas for investigation would be bound to dilute and de-focus effort, and even worse academics would aim for the easiest targets. Anyone who goes to academic conferences regularly is aware of the latter phenomenon.

2. It would emphasize methodology rather than substance. Follow me closely here, this is an esoteric argument. We currently do not have a general theory of marketing, applicable to all forms of marketing, because we have yet to define what marketing really is. In order to create a general theory, we need to focus on research which is generalizable, that is which can be applied in all circumstances. This leads us to focus on theory testing rather than theory building, which in turn tends to emphasize quantitative, positivist research methodologies.

3. It would result in an increasingly esoteric and abstract literature. Allowing the marketing domain to diverge as greatly as it has allows researchers to carry out work in areas which have little or no connection with real-life, everyday marketing issues, as long as they can make some vague connection with exchange theory. Again, I have seen some very weird papers presented at conferences, with correspondingly surreal conversations following on from them.

A survey in 1974 showed that most academic marketers were overwhelmingly in favour of the broadening of the concept to include non-profit marketing, etc. The reasons for this are obscure, but one might suppose that expanding the scope of the marketing domain is akin to expanding the borders of the British Empire: at one time, it just seemed to be the right thing to do. Expanding the boundaries still implies the creation of a new boundary, though, as well as a framework within which we can study the subject (or on which we can hang our findings). One framework which was proposed was that of Hunt (1976). Hunt suggested that all marketing questions can be categorized along three dimensions: macro vs. micro, profit vs. non-profit, and positive vs. normative. Profit vs. non-profit was to be based on whether the organization intended to make a profit or not. Note that this is about intentions – like many other people, I have worked for organizations which were non-profit-making, but that was not the way we wanted it to be. Micro vs. macro refers to the dichotomy between individual suppliers and consumers on the one hand, and groups of suppliers and consumers on the other. Positive vs. normative refers to the dichotomy between describing what already exists and prescribing what should exist.

Having sorted out the dimensions within which we can research marketing questions, we can presumably draw up a matrix to show what kind of research or thinking occupies each of the eight boxes which would appear. This still does not determine absolutely where the boundaries of marketing are or should be, but it does make a nice way of categorizing people's work in the field.

Other academics think that marketing is not, and never can be, a proper science. Because of the huge number of variables inherent in any question of marketing (varying from the fickleness and unpredictability of consumer behaviour to the Machiavellian plotting and treachery of our competitors, customers and suppliers), marketing planning has to be undertaken by guesswork and gut feeling. In other words, it is an art form. Here we need to consider what art is all about, though.

Creating a work of art is not actually the emotional, visceral, intuitive process most people imagine it to be. Artists (and I have known a fair few) are generally pretty good at calculating exactly how they are going to paint the portrait or mould the sculpture, and they have almost always spent a number of years learning precise techniques for doing what they do. So much for the input side of creating art. How about the output side? What is art for? Usually art is said to be a means of conveying ideas or emotions, and it is true that marketing communications often use the techniques and trappings of art to convey ideas and emotions. This is not, however, the whole of marketing: let's not fall into the trap of thinking that marketing is only about advertising and selling, or we will be classing ourselves with the laymen, and that would never do.

My own view is that art is there to make us look at the world in a different way. Is marketing therefore an art? Possibly, because on the input side we certainly plan our activities carefully and have access to a range of techniques and skills which have been acquired with some expense and difficulty. Marketing academics, and indeed practitioners, are often in the position of trying to make people see the company in a different way, that is see it from the customer's viewpoint. Needless to say this doesn't always work. Having said all that, it seems to me that marketing is not art. It may have some of the trappings of art, but the overall effect is not to produce artworks but to produce measurable outcomes, and that puts it firmly in the camp of science.

Marketing is, at present, bad science. The current state of knowledge puts it in the realms of alchemy at best. While we, as academics, look to the wisdom of the ancients to guide us in turning the base metal of selling and advertising into the gold of the marketing concept, practitioners are combining the base elements (price, product, place and promotion) in the hope of creating a new Philosopher's Stone which will open the boardroom door.

why other academics do not respect us

The simple answer is that we are applied, and they are not. The lengthier answer is that they do not have to begin their lecture programmes and textbooks by explaining what the subject is. They are able to rely on a pre-existing knowledge that anyone who signs up for the course will have, that is what the subject is about. In the case of marketing, most people think that it is about advertising or personal selling (because these are the most obvious aspects of marketing to non-marketers), or that it is a function of the business rather than a driving philosophy (which again is frequently true in the real world). Since marketers themselves cannot agree, and since the definitions used by practitioners differ in both content and concept from those used by academics, it is no wonder that we are regarded as a fluffy-bunny subject with no real basis. For example, consider the following.

Kotler defines marketing as follows (Kotler et al., 2003: 10):

> Marketing is a social and managerial process by which individuals and groups obtain what they need and want through creating and exchanging products and value with others.

No mention of profit here, and in fact no mention of marketing as a driving philosophy – simply a practical process. Substitute 'shopping' for 'marketing' and the definition still reads fairly well. Substitute 'business' for marketing and it reads perfectly.

The Chartered Institute of Marketing uses the following definition:

> Marketing is the management process which identifies, anticipates, and supplies customer requirements efficiently and profitably.

Consumers don't apparently figure in the CIM definition, and not-for-profit marketing is clearly not part of their view either. Perhaps more insidiously, it implies that a company which is currently losing money is not engaged in marketing, or (curiouser and curiouser) a company which sells a product below cost as a loss leader or sales promotion is also not engaged in marketing. Management is part of the CIM world, though, which implies that any exchanges which are not managed as part of the process are not part of marketing. Not unreasonable.

Another commonly quoted definition is that provided by the American Marketing Association (2004), as follows:

Marketing is an organizational function and a set of processes for creating, communicating and delivering value to customers and for managing customer relationships in ways that benefit the organization and its stakeholders.

A somewhat more complex definition, this one allows that we might not make a profit. It also talks about managing customer relationships, which is an interesting idea because it sounds very, well, managerial. It sounds as if we are doing things to people again, rather than having a real relationship of equals. Customer centrality implies that it is the customer who manages the relationship, and we'd better mind our Ps and Qs, but especially the Ps. This definition has only recently been arrived at after five years of deliberation, so it must be right. Whether it gives us the boundaries we need is debatable.

Any economist or behavioural scientist looking at the dog's breakfast of definitions we are trying to work with is bound to have doubts as to our seriousness, especially since we profess to be focused on consumers and none of the definitions above include the word 'consumer'. Kotler doesn't even mention customers, which is pretty radical of him.

Drucker (1999) helped us out a little bit here by offering the statement: 'The basic function of marketing is to attract and retain customers at a profit.' Again, this cuts out the non-profit brigade (but not the accidental non-profit marketers – failing at something does not mean that you did not give it your best shot).

The debate about broadening the scope of marketing has given some of us a view that 'everything is marketing and marketing is everything', a concept which is laughable. We can therefore not be too surprised when other academics laugh at us – especially when we can't even agree on a definition.

why marketing practitioners ignore us

My friend and colleague Alan Tapp recently threw a major cat among the pigeons by presenting at a conference, and subsequently publishing, a paper on the topic of practitioner disaffection with marketing academics (Tapp, 2005). In a cogent and well-argued article, Tapp points out that pure research is of scarcely any value at all to practitioners, but applied research has no value in academic circles. The reason for this is that academic research is driven by the Research Assessment Exercise (RAE), which focuses almost entirely on publication in top-rated journals. Since the RAE is a source of funding which does not rely on getting out of bed to teach HND1 at 9 o'clock on a Monday morning, it is highly regarded by university heads of department, and by practically nobody else. The result is that most academics are under pressure to publish, and in particular to get into a 'good' journal.

These journals use a double-blind-review system, which means that the author does not know who the reviewers are, and the reviewers do not know who the author is. Their remit is to maintain the 'standards' of the journal, which almost always means making the journal look as much like a physics journal or a chemistry journal as possible. To do this, the reviewers tend to emphasize research which has been carried out using esoteric statistical tools to generate results, and to use obscure research methodologies to generate conceptual results rather than to report on 'best practice'.

The heavy emphasis on positivist, quantitative studies means that academic papers are increasingly divorced from the realities of human life. We can observe behaviour, but we find it difficult or impossible to discover intentions, since people are often unaware of their own motivations anyway. Consider what happens when we heat a steel bar. The steel expands by an amount which is dependent on the type of steel and the temperature difference. The steel bar doesn't care whether a woman is applying the heat or a man, whether it is in London or Valparaiso, or whether it is Monday morning or Saturday night. Any study involving human beings will be affected greatly by such factors.

Tapp (2005) identifies five ailments which make academic papers irrelevant to practitioners. These are:

1. Researching the obvious.
2. Academia and practice: divided by a common language.

3. Using a multivariate sledgehammer to crack a nut.
4. Researching the obscure or arcane.
5. Ignoring context.

The way to get published in top journals is to use obscure language. Long words and words which sound really scientific are at a premium, and complex sentence construction adds considerably to one's chances of getting published. Here is a direct quote from Tapp's paper, regarding ailments 1 and 2:

> To illustrate this point here's a quote from a recent Top Paper:
>
>> This research demonstrates the positive effects of moment-to-moment entertainment and the negative effects of moment-to-moment information value on consumers' likelihood to continue watching during a television commercial. A notable finding is that both the entertainment value EV and the information value IV have a strong multiplicative effect on the probability to stop viewing.
>
> Once you have chewed your way through the academic jargon (see ailment #2) and turned it into plain English you realize the authors are claiming that ... *if the advert is boring, people are less likely to watch it.* I'm not sure about you, but I'd already filed that one under 'basic common sense'. (Tapp, 2005: 7)

Some of the problems Tapp identifies come from a view that we should be publishing in American journals. This is because the RAE assessors value American journals above European ones. This is a strange concept in a sense, but actually one which comes from two sources. First, there is a common view that marketing was invented by the Americans and therefore they know most about it and have the most perceptive academics. Secondly, there is a powerful driver towards publication in 'international' journals. This driver is translated as publishing in 'foreign' journals. Many European journals would have an international currency were it not that American academics tend to think that they own marketing and therefore Europeans have nothing to tell them, but perhaps I am being a tad cynical.

So why have marketing academics allowed themselves to be railroaded in this way? Why have we allowed the journal reviewers and

RAE assessors (who are themselves marketers) to push us into producing research with little or no value? One is drawn towards the conclusion that it is due to a desire to be recognized as a real science, with real numerical techniques, and real results that no one can understand. The temptation to use words and concepts that no one else understands is a great one – how else can we prove that we are cleverer than everyone else?

Perhaps, as an alternative approach, we could prove it by explaining complex ideas in a way that anyone can understand. Unfortunately, the basic concepts of marketing (as we have seen) are extremely simple, so we are forced into explaining simple things in as convoluted a way as we can.

why the public don't like us

Most people don't like marketers. This is partly because of the black art view of marketing, partly because of a general mistrust of business, and partly because people are aware that they have much less negotiating power than Adam Smith and the average marketing executive would have them believe. It's all very well for Sam Walton, the founder of what is now the world's largest retail company (Wal*Mart) to tell us that 'the customer can fire everybody in the company, from the CEO on down, simply by spending his money elsewhere', but is this really true? How much choice do people really have, when retailers pull cunning stunts like negotiating exclusive deals with manufacturers which prevent said manufacturers selling their goods anywhere else? To what extent can customers choose, when the market is dominated by perhaps four or five companies, none of which has a vested interest in upsetting the status quo?

Consumer trust is not helped by the stated definitions of marketing as being concerned with the profits of the companies. The concept of the enlightened self-interest of major business has had a few knocks in recent years, and certainly the Kotlerite view that the greatest good of society can be realized by the profitability of large corporations is somewhat bizarre. Quite obviously the best interests of a large organization are served by short-term rape and pillage, not by nurturing the world's resources and preserving them for future competitors. Granted, too short-term a view creates problems of its own, but in general it is better to grab it while you can.

Marketers have great difficulty in dispelling these perceptions, not least because there is a measure of truth in them. However, we have also seen the results of trying to control people's consumption and production by state intervention: Eastern European communism provided some benefits at first, but quickly degenerated into a free-for-all in which Party commissars ended up with the best houses, cars and job opportunities, and everyone else lived on cabbages. The current view of economic control is that it does not work. The best and safest approach is now thought to be the free market, with suitable controls in place to ensure a minimum of rapaciousness. Pardon me while I say 'Oh, yeah?'

As always, the problem is that we have an imperfect world, but we have little knowledge of how to remove or at least mitigate its imperfections. We are operating under the best conditions we can manage, and using the current best theory, but there is not a shadow of a doubt that we will be using new theories in a few years' time. Where are these new theories to come from? Perhaps (breathe it softly) the real scientific investigations carried out by marketing academics and others.

why marketing doesn't work

This is the chapter heading, so I owe you an apology for recycling it. On the other hand, you need a section which explains why marketing has not fulfilled its early promise.

In the 1960s the world was (surprisingly) feeling pretty good about itself, despite the Cold War and the nuclear tests and so forth. We were feeling good about ourselves because we thought we had a vision of a bright future (even though some of us were having visions of giant red butterflies fluttering across the sky). Industry was going to provide us with everything we needed, the economy was going to keep growing, and we were all going to love each other and give each other flowers. As marketing grew to be more mainstream, it took on these ideas: look after the customers and they will look after you; meet people's needs better than your competitors do and they (the people) will love you for it.

Unfortunately, the truth was somewhat different. Marketers offered customers more and more, and in exchange were simply pressured to provide even more: the exceptional became commonplace, and expectations rose. We simply taught consumers to be greedy and demanding, like spoiled children. The major American car manufacturers competed to provide ever-larger, ever better-equipped, ever more opulent vehicles. What happened? The Japanese entered the US market with smaller, cheaper, more economical cars and clobbered the big manufacturers.

Airlines offer another example. Major airlines offered more comfortable seating, more legroom, better in-flight meals, faster check-ins in an effort to outperform their rivals. Customers ate the in-flight meals, ogled the stewardesses, drank the free booze, watched the in-flight movies, and then booked with easyJet next time because it's cheaper. There's no in-flight meal, and you have to have a punch-up with your fellow passengers to get a window seat, but hey, it's half the price!

We have had nearly forty years of marketing academics teaching students to differentiate, segment, find the USP, add value, and even (oo-er) delight the customer, and what do customers do? Buy the cheapest. Adam Smith must be chortling away to himself somewhere.

Where does this leave us? Do we end up like the Americans, where restaurant customers have the effrontery to tell the chef how to cook their dinners, or do we stay with the European model, in which we expect the chef to know about food, and present us with it accordingly? Which is closer to the marketing concept? Which is the most customer-orientated? Most importantly, which would you prefer?

If you choose the 'chef is the expert' option, you are espousing the product concept. If you choose the easyJet option, you are espousing the production concept. Only if you choose the American option will you be choosing the marketing concept, and I suspect that that way lies perdition. It's one thing for customers to demand that the chef leaves out the salt and holds the mayo, it's quite another for airline passengers to tell the pilot how to fly the plane. Yet the two are not too far apart. What happens when we allow students to decide how a course should be run? The average student is going to want to be told what the answers are to the exam questions, and nothing else (I would be the same – this isn't an attack on students). We would all rather have just been given the piece of paper (the degree or whatever) on enrolment day and cut out all that late-night studying. But luckily students *don't* run the courses and we end up with them actually learning to think a bit (we hope). This tends to lead us back to a managerial definition of marketing – that the providers should manage the process with the best interests of the consumer at heart – rather than the Adam Smith 'consumer is king' definition.

The other major stumbling block for applying the marketing concept is that it is not in the best interests of the decision-makers themselves. Company directors are not Mother Theresa: they are not any more altruistic than the rest of us (though most of the company directors I have known have been no less altruistic, on average, than the rest of us). A Board of Directors often acts as a clearing-house for pressures rather than a dictatorship, so directors need to consider the needs of a wide range of stakeholders, not just the customers. They are well aware that a business is made up of people, some of whom are valuable and must be retained, some of whom are vociferous and must be appeased, and some of whom are past their sell-by date and either need to be re-motivated or need to be got rid of. From a director's viewpoint, there is simply no case for preferring one group of stakeholders over another, particularly when one group (employees) is intending to be around for the long term and customers are notoriously fickle. From a strictly legal viewpoint, in fact, directors are required to act in the best interests of the shareholders, and can be brought to account if they fail to do so.

At a more personal level, from the viewpoint of a director, the purpose of a company is not profit. Companies are put on this planet by a munificent deity for the directors to have fun. They can hire people, fire people, ride around in the company limousine (or the company jet, if they're lucky), make decisions, and generally be Very Busy and Important People. The view from lower down the ladder is that the company is about earning a salary and paying the mortgage – directors of large companies have, in the main, gone well beyond worrying about the mortgage.

For example, in 2003 Kate Swann moved from her job as managing director of Argos to take over the reins of the troubled stationers, WH Smith. She was reputed to have been given a 'golden hello' worth £2.4 million in total, and a salary of £475,000 a year. This is not someone whose future financial planning is based on buying scratchcards. At the age of 38, she need have no worries about her finances. So why do it? Why not stay home and keep away from the stress and hoopla of running a large company? Simple – it's exciting to take a firm that's in trouble and turn it round so that it is profitable.

So does marketing work? Well, in order for us to be able to say whether marketing works or not, we need to be able to say what it was supposed to do in the first place. Marketers have moved their views on this so much it has become difficult for outsiders (and insiders for that matter) to get a clear image of what we are playing at. Are we about doing the customers a drop of good? A surprising number of academics seem to think so. Are we about creating profits? The CIM seem to think so. Are we about managing exchange? Bagozzi and Kotler seem to think so. Are we about meeting organizational objectives and managing relationships? The American Marketing Association seem to think so.

If you cast your mind back to Chapter 3, you may recall Peter Doyle's ideas on shareholder value as the driving force for corporate strategy. Unless marketers fall into line with the rest of the corporate management on this issue, we will be left outside the Board Room door with a packet of crisps and a glass of lemonade until we are grown up enough to join the real business world.

▩▩▩▩   why marketing can be a real science, so there

Marketing academics are understandably unlikely to admit that what they are doing is not real science. Despite Alan Tapp's well-argued criticisms, some very good research is carried out by marketers, and some very real, practical results are obtained. For example, it was academic marketers who discovered that people who are in the room while the TV advertisements are on have several different responses, ranging from zapping the ad to see what's on the other channels through to interacting with the ads (singing the jingles, guessing the product, and so forth). Practitioners had previously made the ludicrous assumption that people in the room actually watched the ads, an assumption which they didn't believe themselves, but which it would have been professional suicide to ignore. Academics are good at cutting through these 'emperor's new clothes' scenarios because they have no vested interest, at least not in the world of the practitioner.

Secondly, although the criticism has been levelled that marketing is derived from practice, and all the theoretical 'pure' work belongs up there with economics and behavioural sciences, marketers still have plenty to do at the interface between the social sciences. As a form of behavioural economics, or economic psychology, marketing (as an academic subject) may be able to carve out a niche.

Thirdly, the physical sciences, at the highest conceptual level, operate by observing and analysing phenomena in the real world, and formulating generalizable theories to explain what they observe. These basic principles can as easily be applied to market phenomena as to astronomical phenomena or chemical phenomena: if we want to call this research into marketing, then why should we not do so?

Several writers have tried to outline a general set of rules for theory building. One favourite is Dubin (1978), who developed the following model:

1. A theoretical model starts with variables or units whose interactions constitute the subject matter of attention.

2. The model specifies the ways in which these units interact with each other.
3. This develops the laws of interaction.
4. Since theoretical models necessarily consider only parts of reality, the theory must include the boundaries within which the theory is expected to hold true.
5. Most theoretical models are presumed to represent a complex portion of the real world.
6. This complexity is revealed by the fact that there are various system states, in each of which the units react differently with each other.
7. The theorist should then be in a position to derive conclusions that represent logical and true deductions about the model or the propositions of the model.

As we have seen, marketing has trouble with deciding what its units are and where its boundaries lie, which naturally makes life difficult for the theory builder. Developing a rigorous theory of marketing would still not be straightforward, even if the boundaries were agreed, because most marketing academics are former practitioners and want to carry out practical, usable research rather than engage in abstruse theory-building.

Robert Morgan of Cardiff University is one of the many academics who believes that marketing is a real science, so there. In a paper published in 1996 he explains that marketing theory has three components: systematically related themes, lawlike generalizations, and empirical testability. He regards the first two components as being basic to any scientific study, and points to the wealth of published research in marketing as evidence of the empirical testing of theory. The main danger he perceives is that the multitude of topics all studied under the generic label of marketing has led to a fragmentation of the theory. This may be evidence that the boundaries are still not in place for the discipline as a whole – which is where we came in.

Shelby Hunt (see Chapter 3) contributed a positivist view of marketing theory which has since been substantially criticized (as most positivist views have been criticized). A brief aside about positivism is indicated here. Basically, positivists believe that the truth is out there, that we can discover universal laws of how the world works and explain reality. Positivism derives from the physical sciences. The assumption is that a detached researcher can carry out an experiment (for example, heat up a steel bar) and observe a phenomenon (the bar expands) which would be observable by any other researcher who carries out the same experiment. As we saw earlier in the chapter, it does not matter if the researchers are male or female, old or young, or if the research is carried out in Scunthorpe or Valparaiso. The results will be the same. This is fine for physicists, but people are not steel bars.

For social scientists, positivism has been brought into disrepute in recent years, and interpretivist approaches have become much more common. Interpretivists do not believe that the researcher and the research can be separated, or that general laws of society can be worked out. Any theory is only true for a specific place and time, and while it may be informative for dealing with similar situations in future, it ain't set in concrete.

So well-established is this view, in Europe at least, that I have heard presenters at conferences apologise for being positivists. American academics remain substantially positivist, however, probably because the majority of physical scientists are positivists and we envy them their respectability. There are rumblings among physical scientists, though. Some are adopting the epistemological view that reality is subject to multiple interpretations, and that therefore positivism may not apply in the physical sciences either. If this view becomes widespread, there's no knowing what chaos may result.

Since marketing is an inherently chaotic 'science', interpretivism offers a way out. We can still be proper scientists, but we don't have to develop laws and bodies of theory – just temporary theories to explain temporary observations. Phew, that's a relief! The only problem is, the major journals may not publish us, and we may not make it through the Research Assessment Exercise. Apart from affecting the university's funding, this outcome can have a bad effect on one's career prospects.

so what *is* marketing?

So we are still left with the first lecture/first chapter question in Introduction to Marketing: What is marketing? Often, we know what it isn't, and we base our definitions on that. It isn't just selling, it isn't just advertising, it isn't just PR. It may be a philosophical paradigm for decision-making within the firm (is this decision going to connect us more closely to our customers?), or it may be a tactical function (is looking after this group of customers going to increase our shareholder value?), or it may be simply a set of activities which somebody has to do if we are going to shift product (will this ad campaign bring in a few more suckers?). It may even turn out to be a black art by which wicked capitalists manipulate innocent consumers.

The debate is apt to continue for some time. My own view is that marketing is actually a means to an end rather than an end in itself, so I am in the 'tactical function' camp I suppose. As a former practitioner, and a relatively new academic, I suppose I am not really too interested in deeper philosophical arguments about research and theory-building: I want to find out quick answers that will work for the time being, not develop deep theories which last for centuries. Life's too short.

Other people have other views. Most academics would like marketing to become a proper science, and they seek to build a general theory of marketing which will rank with general theories of physics, chemistry, or biology. If we even get to be as well regarded as economics, we will be doing well, of course. At the same time, practitioners would like marketing to be a strategic paradigm, a philosophy for running the business: this is the only way we'll get marketers in the board rooms, where currently they are somewhat rare creatures.

Meanwhile, whatever camp you end up in and whatever use you make of your insights into marketing, it is a field of study which provides endless fascination and opportunities for debate. It's an exciting field, populated by some eccentric and entertaining creatures, whether they be rebellious academics or flamboyant over-confident practitioners. May it be a field that you enjoy striding about in – even if parts of it are sometimes muddied.

Epilogue

Marketing, it is said, is a young discipline. One might say that marketing is so undisciplined it acts like a two-year-old, rather than the 250-year-old it actually is, but the point is that we are still debating what marketing is, where it has come from, where its boundaries lie, and where it is going. This makes it as lively as a basketful of kittens, and as immediate as a punch in the nose. Young disciplines are like that.

One of the great things about marketing is that there is always more to learn. Okay, it's a cliché – but like most clichés, it only became a cliché because people liked the sound of it and it rings true. Marketing, as an academic subject and as a practical profession, changes all the time. There is a saying in academic circles that all the lecturers have to write new exam papers every year except the marketers: all the marketers have to do is change the answers. Practitioners are told that they should always be trying to do something different from the competition: if marketing had a motto, it would be 'New Improved'.

Anyway, I hope you enjoyed the book. I enjoyed writing it. It isn't often a publisher lets me loose to write anything I fancy; we usually have reviewers and lecturers and templates and deadlines which mean I have to do as I'm told. The ideas in the book were sometimes mine, but mostly they were other people's and I just added my little bit of commentary. I hope you (and they) don't mind too much.

References

American Marketing Association (2004) www.marketingpower.com

Anderson, J.C. & Soderlund, M. (1988) 'The network approach to marketing', *Irish Marketing Review*, 3: 63–8.

Bartels, Robert (1976) *The History of Marketing Thought*. Columbus, OH: Grid Inc.

Borden, N. (1964) 'The concept of the marketing mix', *Journal of Advertising Research*, June: 2–7.

Doyle, P. (2000) *Value-based Marketing*. Chichester: John Wiley.

Drucker, P.F. (1954) *The Practice of Management*. New York: HarperCollins.

Drucker, P.F. (1973) *Management*. New York: Harper & Row.

Drucker, P.F. (1999) 'Knowledge-worker productivity: the biggest challenge', *California Management Review*, 41: 79–94.

Dubin, R. (1978) *Theory Building*. New York: Free Press.

Edgeworth, F.Y. (1881) *Mathematical Psychics: An Essay on the Application of Mathematics to the Moral Sciences*. London: Kogan Paul & Co.

Ehrenberg, A.S.C. (1974) 'Repetitive advertising and the consumer', *Journal of Advertising Research*, 14 (2): 25–34.

Ehrenberg, A.S.C. (1988) *Repeat Buying: Facts, Theory and Applications*. London: Charles Griffin.

Festinger, L. & Carlsmith, J. Merrill (1959) 'Cognitive consequences of forced compliance', *Journal of Abnormal and Social Psychology*, 58: 203–10.

Firat, A.F. & Schultz, C.J. (1997) 'From segmentation to fragmentation: markets and marketing strategy in the postmodern era', *European Journal of Marketing*, 31 (3/4): 183–207.

Frey, A.W. (1961) *Advertising* (3rd edition). New York: The Ronald Press.

Friedman, M. (2002 [1962]) *Capitalism and Freedom*. Chicago, IL: University of Chicago Press.

Fullerton, Ronald (1988) 'How modern is modern marketing? Marketing's evolution and the myth of the production era', *Journal of Marketing*, 52 (1) January: 108–15.

Gibson, J.J. (1977) 'The Theory of Affordances', in R. Shaw & J. Bransford (eds), *Perceiving, Acting and Knowing*. Hillsdale, NJ: Erlbaum.

Gilbert, D.C. & Bailey, N. (1990) 'The development of marketing: a compendium of historical approaches', *Quarterly Review of Marketing*, 15 (2): 6–13.

Goffman, E. (1959) *The Presentation of Self in Everyday Life*. New York: Anchor Books.

Herzberg, F. (1966) *Work and the Nature of Man*. London: William Collins.

Hicks, David & Gwynne, Margaret A. (1996) *Cultural Anthropology*. New York: HarperCollins.

Hofstede, G. (1984) *Culture's Consequences: International Differences in Work-related Values*. Beverley Hills, CA: Sage.

Howard, J.A. (1957) *Marketing Management: Analysis and Planning*. Homewood, IL: Irwin.

Howard, J.A. and Sheth, J.N. (1969) *The Theory of Buyer Behavior*. New York: John Wiley.

Hunt, S.D. (1976) 'The nature and scope of marketing', *Journal of Marketing*, 40, 3 (July): 17–28.

Hunt, S.D. (1983) *Marketing Theory: The Philosophy of Marketing Science*. Homewood, IL: Irwin.

Keith, Robert J. (1960) 'The marketing revolution', *Journal of Marketing*, 24 (January): 35–8.

Kent, R.A. (1986) 'Faith in the 4Ps: an alternative', *Journal of Marketing Management*, 2 (2): 145–54.

Keynes, J.M. (1960 [1936]) *The General Theory of Employment, Interest and Money*. London: Palgrave Macmillan.

Kotler, P. & Levy, Sidney J. (1969) 'Broadening the concept of marketing', *Journal of Marketing*, 33 (January): 10–15.

Kotler, P., Armstrong, G., Saunders, J. & Wong, V. (2003) *Principles of Marketing*. Harlow: Prentice Hall.

Lazer, W. & Kelly, E.J. (1962) *Managerial Marketing: Perspectives and Viewpoints*. Homewood, IL: Irwin.

Levitt, T. (1960) 'Marketing myopia', *Harvard Business Review*, 38: 45–56.

Levitt, T. (1983) 'After the sale is over', *Harvard Business Review*, September–October.

Luck, D.J. (1969) 'Broadening the Concept of Marketing – Too Far', *Journal of Marketing*, 33 (July): 53–5.

Maguire, Eleanor A., Frackowiak, Richard S.J. & Frith, Christopher D. (1997) 'Recalling routes around London: activation of the right hippocampus in taxi drivers', *Journal of Neuroscience*, 17: 7103–10

Malthus, Thomas (1992 [1798]) *An Essay on the Principle of Population, as it Affects the Future Improvement of Society with Remarks on the Speculations of Mr. Godwin, M. Condorcet, and Other Writers*. Oxford: Oxford University Press.

Marshall, A. (1997 [1890]) *Principles of Economics*. New York: Prometheus Books.

Marx, K. (1993 [1867]) *Capital: A Critique of Political Economy*. Harmondsworth: Penguin Books.

Maslow, A. (1954) *Motivation and Personality*. New York: Harper & Row.

McCarthy, E.J. (1960) *Basic Marketing: A Managerial Approach*. Homewood, IL: Irwin.

McCarthy, E.J. and Perreault, W.D. (2004) *Basic Marketing* (15th edition). Maidenhead: McGraw-Hill.

McLuhan, H.M. (1964) *Understanding Media: The Extensions of Man*. New York: Signet Books.

Mead, M. (1935) *Sex and Temperament in Three Primitive Societies*. New York: Wiley.

Mill, J.S. (1998 [1848]) *The Principles of Political Economy*. Oxford: Oxford University Press.

Morgan, Robert E. (1996) 'Conceptual foundations of marketing and marketing theory', *Management Decision*, 34 (10): 19–26.

Morgan, R.M. & Hunt, S.D. (1994) 'The Commitment–trust theory of relationship marketing', *Journal of Marketing*, 58(3): 20–38.

Muniz, Albert M. Jr. & O'Guinn, Thomas C. (2001) 'Brand community', *Journal of Consumer Research*, 27, 4 (March): 412–32.

Peters, T. & Waterman, R.H. (1982) *In Search of Excellence*. New York: Harper & Row.

Petty, Richard E. & Caccioppo, John T. (1983) 'Central and peripheral routes to persuasion: application to advertising', in Larry Percy & Arch Woodside (eds), *Advertising and Consumer Psychology*. Lexington, MA: Lexington Books.

Pohl, F. & Kornbluth, C.M. (2003 [1953]) *The Space Merchants*. London: Victor Gollancz.

Ricardo, D. (1992 [1817]) *Principles of Political Economy and Taxation*. New York: Prometheus Books.

Rosengren, K.E. (1999) *Communication: An Introduction*. London: Sage.

Schramm, W. (ed.) (1948) *Communication in Modern Society*. Urbana, IL: University of Illinois Press.

Sheth, J. & Sisodia, R. (2002) *The Rule of Three: Surviving and Thriving in Competitive Markets*. New York: Free Press.

Smith, Adam (1998 [1776]) *Wealth of Nations*. Oxford: Oxford Paperbacks

Tapp, A. (2005) 'Why practitioners don't read our articles and what we should do about it', *The Marketing Review*, 5 (1): 3–13.

Tynan, C. (1997) 'A review of the marriage analogy in relationship marketing', *Journal of Marketing Management*, 13 (7): 695–703.

Vroom, V.H. (1964) *Work and Motivation*. New York: John Wiley.

Walras, Leon (1984 [1874]) *Elements of Pure Economics*. London: Porcupine Press.

Warhol, Andy (1975) *The Philosophy of Andy Warhol: From A to B and Back Again*. New York: Harcourt Brace Jovanovich.

Index